THE
HELP YOURSELF
COOKBOOK FOR KIDS

THE HELP YOURSELF

COOKBOOK FOR KIDS

60+ EASY PLANt-BASED RECIPES
KIDS CAN MAKE tO STAY
HEALtHY AND SAVE the WORLD

WRittEN & ILLUSTRAtED

by RUBY ROTH

Andrews McMeel
Publishing®
a division of Andrews McMeel Universal

CONTENTS

INTRODUCTION
A NOTE FROM THE AUTHOR

"Tell me and I forget, teach me and I may remember, involve me and I learn."
—Anonymous

Probably since you were born, someone has been making your meals and feeding you (that's the life!). But wait a minute...what's that there on the end of your arm?! Why, it's a **HELPING HAND!**

You, _____, are a very strong and capable person. You have a **LOT** of power! You hardly need anything more than your own two hands and a few ingredients to help save the world (and feed yourself)! This book is called *Help Yourself* because it turns out that helping yourself to healthy food actually helps animals and the planet, too.

(Your name here)

The recipes in this book are **VEGAN**, which means they use only ingredients that come from plants—no animals or animal products.

Here's the deal: From the tip of your nose to the tip of an iceberg, the foods we eat affect our bodies, animals, the environment, and even strangers on the other side of the planet.

It sounds impossible, but it's the truth.

HOW EATING PLANTS CAN HELP SAVE THE WORLD:

1. Plant foods help us stay healthy.

2. Growing plants uses up less land, water, and energy than raising animals does (and causes less pollution, too).

3. No animals suffer when we eat plants.

4. Plants can feed more people around the world than meat or dairy can.

5. Plants contain more nutrients than animal products do.

Aaand...making meals out of plant foods is like doing an art project—but instead of glue, scissors, and paint, you've got THIS to play with!

Read the recipes, but feel free to be creative and use your imagination, too!

Remember, we are all connected. If we make the 🌍 a happier, kinder, cleaner, safer place for all, life gets better for us, too.

I believe in you. Now go...HELP YOURSELF!

—Ruby Roth

MEET SOME INGREDIENTS

One minute these foods are new—the next minute they're old favorites! They are all easy to find at health food stores, more and more at big-name grocery stores, and online if you want them delivered to your door—and they last a long time. Once you buy them, you'll use them a LOT in this book. See Resources (page 118) for my favorite brands.

AGAVE Similar to maple syrup, which comes from a maple tree, agave is a sweet syrup that comes from a cactus—nature is so cool, right? Your body soaks up agave much more slowly than sugar, so you won't go so crazy when you eat it.

ALGAE are tiny plants that grow in ponds and lakes, and are some of nature's most perfect foods, containing a high amount of protein, plus a long list of vitamins, minerals, and nutrients for your energy, heart, blood, eyes, brain, and immune system. Algae are dried and ground to a powder and can be found in the vitamin section of health food stores or online. A bottle can *seem* expensive, but it lasts a *very* long time, so each nutritious use costs only a few cents. Algae are super helpful for your nutrition and health. We use two kinds in this book:

BLUE-GREEN ALGAE are named for their beautiful color. Get as much in your body as you can by sprinkling the algae in juices, water (they will turn it the most beautiful turquoise!), on salads, in chocolate recipes, or in guacamole.

SPIRULINA is named for its shape: under a microscope it looks like tiny spirals. This green-black powder is fun to sprinkle on everything from smoothies to popcorn because it turns everything green.

ALMOND FLOUR is simply almonds ground into a powder. One package goes a long way, and we use it in several recipes in this book. Plus, it's good sprinkled on everything from fruit bowls to ice cream, yogurt, or oatmeal, or in smoothies.

BOUILLON CUBES are little squares of oil, herbs, and salt, all packed together. They melt into soups to make them super tasty and flavorful. NOTE: Most bouillon is made with palm oil, which often comes from farms that destroy forests to plant their crops, but I use Rapunzel brand because it's vegan, organic, fair-trade, habitat-friendly, and sustainable (I wrote to them to find out). You can find Rapunzel cubes in health food stores or online. Once you get the hang of making the soups in this book, you can flavor them with dried or fresh herbs, garlic, salt, and a drizzle of oil instead. Toss the herbs into the soup loose, or pack a large handful into a mesh spice ball and soak it inside the pot of soup as it cooks.

BRAGG LIQUID AMINOS (Bragg's for short) looks and tastes like soy sauce (see shoyu, page xii). It gives soups, salads, and sauces a yummy salty flavor and is full of healthy amino acids (proteins). I always have it in my kitchen and we will use it a LOT in this book. You can find it at nearly every health food store.

CACAO (rhymes with ka-POW) is the seed of the fruit of chocolate tree—yes, chocolate grows on trees! Raw cacao isn't sweet on its own, but has the chocolaty taste we all love and is one of the most nutritious foods on the planet, with lots of antioxidants (cell protectors), vitamins, and minerals, like magnesium, iron, vitamin C, and omega-6. Lucky us! We use it mostly in powder form in this book, but you can buy cacao powder, whole beans, or nibs (crushed up pieces)

from any health food store. NOTE: Look for RAW cacao powder, not cocoa (CO-co), which is usually heated and mixed with other ingredients—not nearly as nutritious.

CHIA SEEDS are tiny white or black seeds that contain special healthy fats called omegas. Along with beans and corn, chia seeds were one of the main foods of the ancient Aztec people, who ate them for strength and energy, and as medicine, too. Chia is easy to find at many grocery stores, any health food store, or online.

COCONUT We use dried coconut a lot in this book—it comes from the white "meat" inside the coconut. Find it in the bulk or baking sections of a grocery store—shredded (which works best for Grass Shacks, page 113) or in larger flakes for recipes you might eat with your fingers, like Granola Crumble, page 38, or Blaze a Trail, page 28. If the recipe just says "dried coconut," choose which shape you like best. Coconut is full of healthy fats that also help soak up other nutrients and deliver them to your cells.

COCONUT OIL is the oil squeezed from coconut "meat" and is a healthy fat that protects our cells, feeds our brains, balances our hormones (the body's messengers), and helps us fight viruses, germs, and bacteria. Look for "cold-pressed."

GOJI BERRIES are as popular in Asia as raisins are in North America, and now they're becoming better known around the world. Chewy and sweet, they are jam-packed with good stuff! By weight, gojis have more vitamin C than oranges, more beta-carotene than carrots, and more iron than spinach!

HEMP SEEDS are soft little moonlike seeds full of every essential amino acid (protein) a human needs! What's so special about the nutrients in hemp seeds is that they are very *bio-available* ("bio" = "life"), meaning your body soaks up and uses these proteins better than those in meat or dairy. Hemp seeds also have an excellent balance of the healthy fats omega-3s and omega-6s, which power your brain.

MOCHI is a dough made from rice (use the brown kind). Find it in the refrigerated section of health food stores. (It comes in hard, flat blocks.) When baked, it becomes a puffy pastry and can be topped with anything you want, sweet or savory. It is wheat-free and gluten-free.

NUTRITIONAL YEAST is a flaky yellow powder with a cheesy taste. It's full of important nutrients, especially B12. In the olden days, people got B12 from eating food grown in soil nutritious with good bacteria, but today's soil isn't as rich, and many people (both meat-eaters and vegans) don't get enough B12. Nutritional yeast helps keep your B12 levels up. We use it almost every day on salads, soups, bean and veggie dishes, even popcorn.

QUINOA (*KEEN-wa*) is a cute little grain with every kind of protein a human being needs, plus many other important vitamins and minerals. It cooks fast and it's available in most grocery stores these days. Easy!

SEAWEEDS Yes, these are plants you see floating in the ocean! Nori (or laver), kombu (or kelp), palm, arame, hijiki, and wakame are all different kinds of edible seaweeds. People in Japan, Korea, and China have eaten seaweed for thousands of years (it's what's wrapped around sushi rolls), and now Americans are catching on to the fact that seaweeds are not only delicious, they are full of protein, vitamins, minerals, and important nutrients like iodine. Seaweed snacks are little packages of roasted and salted nori sheets. You can find seaweeds and seaweed snacks at Whole Foods, Trader Joe's, Costco, and any health food or Asian food store.

SHOYU is the Japanese name for soy sauce. It tastes a little stronger than Bragg Liquid Aminos, but you can use it instead of Bragg's if you like. Look for nama shoyu, which is raw and more nutritious than regular shoyu.

STEVIA is nature's candy without any sugar at all. The little green leaves of a stevia plant taste *ten times* sweeter than sugar, yet even people with diabetes can eat it! Buy it in powder or liquid form at any health food store...and try growing some in your backyard!

TAHINI is a soft spread like peanut butter but made from sesame seeds. It can taste bitter by itself, but when you mix it into recipes, it completely transforms into a creamy, nutty flavor. You'll find it near the nut butters at the grocery store.

TEMPEH is soybeans that have been fermented (aged) and smashed together. It's full of protein, and you can do lots with it because it soaks up the flavor of whatever you put on it. In this book, we use it to replace fish in the Pretend Tuna Salad (page 70). Find it in the refrigerated section of your health food store (it comes in flat blocks).

TURMERIC is a root that looks like ginger on the outside and carrot on the inside. It's sold as a beautiful yellow-orange powdered spice known for its antioxidant (cell-protecting) and anti-inflammatory powers (this means it reduces pain). It's a very good non-spicy spice to play with—it turns everything golden yellow!

NUMBER ONE RULE: You must have an adult's permission to work in the kitchen, or we'll both get a time-out! Here are things a grown-up can teach you so that eventually, you can use this book on your own. Until then, get some help so you don't lose a finger, or **EVEN WORSE,** burn the meal you were so excited to eat. And anyway, even *expert* cooks have assistants, too, called *sous* ("soo") *chefs.*

• CHOP CHOP!

Carefully practice using a knife. Curl the hand holding the food so your fingertips grasp the food item and your knuckles push against the *side* of the knife's blade. As the knife goes up and down, your fingertips will be out of the way, see? When chopping anything round—say, an onion—first cut it in half, then lay the flat side down to cut the rest.

• TOOLS OF THE TRADE

Besides **MEASURING SPOONS AND CUPS** and **MIXING BOWLS,** a few kitchen tools make preparing great food very easy. A **POWERFUL BLENDER** like a Blendtec or Vitamix (which has a plunger that helps *mix* what's inside the blender *while it's on*) is super helpful for making vegan food. If you have a regular blender, you may just have to start and stop it more often to scrape down the sides with a spatula. If you have a **FOOD PROCESSOR,** you can use that, too. A **SALAD SPINNER** is also helpful to wash, dry, and store greens. If you don't have one, wash greens in a colander and shake them dry or pat them with a clean kitchen towel.

• TURN UP THE HEAT! BOILING VS. SIMMERING

Practice using the stovetop by heating a pot of water. Turn the heat to **HIGH** to bring the water to a boil (big, fast bubbles) and to **MEDIUM** to simmer (slower, smaller bubbles). Also, for recipes at the stove, use a step stool. You want to be steady and balanced so you don't fall into the pot yourself. (After all, we do not cook animals in this book—that includes you!)

• DING! TIME IS UP!

To make sure nothing gets burned (including your house), it's *always* smart to use a timer when you're cooking to remind you when to turn off the heat.

• COME CLEAN!

Wash your hands and fingernails before cooking (who *knows* where they've been) and rinse your fruits and veggies before use.

• MEASURING & MEASUREMENTS

The measurements in this book are here to guide you, but you can change them as you learn what you like. In this book, I use a little less of certain strong ingredients (like garlic or green onions) than I normally would. If you like them, you can always add more.

At first, follow the measurements. (If it says $\frac{1}{4}$ teaspoon, fill the $\frac{1}{4}$ teaspoon to the top!) But after tasting a finished recipe, feel free to add to or change it! If you accidentally put too much of one thing in, just add a little more of the others to balance it out. Once you get the hang of these recipes (and *memorize* about how much a tablespoon, teaspoon, and cup measure), you'll hardly need to use measuring tools at all. You'll know how the meal should look, feel, and taste—and then you can make larger portions by heart! If you're sharing with others, simply double, triple, or quadruple the recipe to make enough for all.

Some ingredients won't even have measurements—that means I'm leaving the amount up to you (for example, how much cinnamon you want on your toast...some like a lot, some like a little—you decide). Other measurements are loose, like "a handful." If you *must* know, here's what I mean:

Giant handful = about $\frac{1}{2}$ to 1 cup

Small handful = $\frac{1}{4}$ to 1/3 cup

Drizzle = a light zigzag pour

Swirl = a quick pour in one circular motion

"MINE"
A LETTER TO GROWN-UPS

Be honest. You might be ambivalent about inviting your kids into the kitchen—into your domain, potentially breaking stuff, definitely making a mess, using up ingredients you planned to cook with, shrieking with delight at flour explosions (don't worry—there's no white flour in this book!). Cooking and cleaning might be *your* thing, a meditative time to yourself. Or, on the other hand, maybe it's something you just want to get through quickly...and by quickly, you mean alone.

I understand. In our house, the kitchen is *my* domain and my hackles prickle when other people start *doing stuff* in there.

However. We want the next generation to eat right, make wise choices, and be conscientious, responsible, and self-sufficient adults. A truly sustainable future lies in actively engaging our children. This is more about ADULTS BEING WILLING to share than it is about any child's ability to learn. So let your kids PLAY with this book. TRUST them. In my experience, when we give kids the information they need to make educated choices, they choose wisely.

A plant-based diet—more broadly, veganism—is about protecting the things we love and value. The benefits extend even beyond the practicalities of health and saving animals and the environment, to our behavior in the world.

Teaching our children to be thoughtful and to consider how their choices affect the public realm will raise the standards for every living being. Because, like our kitchens, the 🌍 is better served when we think of it as "ours," rather than "mine."

—Ruby Roth

I'M THIRSTY
DRINKS

Most junk-food drinks are made with dyes, fake flavors, and chemical colorings—gross. Let's get REAL. Add a little color to the water you drink every day with NATURAL ingredients—now that's a BRIGHT IDEA.

BRIGHT WATERS

SERVES 1 OR 2

FRESH & CLEAN:

5 or more CUCUMBER SLICES

BASIL and/or MINT LEAVES, PINCHED TO RELEASE FLAVOR (OR 1 MINT TEABAG)

BLUE LAGOON:

A SPRINKLE of BLUE-GREEN ALGAE

TICKLED PINK:

3 or more STRAWBERRIES, SLICED

MAGENTA JUICE:
2 or more RAW BEET SLICES

GREEN LAGOON:
A SPRINKLE of SPIRULINA

MELLOW YELLOW:
3 or more LEMON SLICES
CHAMOMILE
(DRIED FLOWERS OR 1 TEABAG)

Place your choice of ingredients in a glass jar with a cap. If you're using berries, gently crush them with a spoon. Add about **1** cup water.

Cap the jar, and SHAKE, SHAKE, SHAKE!

You can drink it right away or let it soak in the fridge overnight. You can also sweeten your drink with a few dashes of stevia powder or a little agave. **NOTE:** If you want your Bright Water to be perfectly clear, pour it through a fine-mesh strainer into your glass just before you drink it.

YOU'LL NEED **FULL BRAIN POWER** IF YOU'RE GOING TO SAVE THE WORLD.

WHEN YOUR BODY GETS THIRSTY, YOUR BRAIN ACTUALLY SHRINKS! DRINK **LOTS** OF WATER TO STAY HYDRATED

DEWDROP
CHIA LEMONADE SERVES 1 or 2

1 CUP WATER

2 TABLESPOONS LEMON JUICE

1½ TABLESPOONS CHIA SEEDS

A HEAPING ½ teaspOON STEViA POWDER (TWO 1-GRAM PACKETS)
OR 1½ TABLESPOONS AGAVE

Put everything in a jar, cap it tightly, and SHAKE, SHAKE, SHAKE it to REALLY mix up the chia seeds. Leave the jar in the fridge for AT LEAST 20 minutes (a few hours or overnight will taste even better). The chia seeds will turn into tiny, jelly-like dewdrops with a seed in the middle. SHAKE, SHAKE, SHAKE them up again and chew as you sip!

NOTE: Depending on how sour your lemons are, you might want to adjust the flavors. When the chia is done soaking, taste and see! Too sour? Add stevia or agave. Too sweet? Add lemon. A little too strong? Add some water. This is what being a CHEF is about!

4

STEVIA COMES FROM A SWEET-LEAFED PLANT, AND AGAVE FROM CACTUS—NO HONEYBEES HARMED! EXPERIMENT WITH OTHER CRUELTY-FREE SWEETENERS—MAPLE OR YACON SYRUP, BEE FREE HONEE, COCONUT SUGAR, BROWN RICE SYRUP, ORGANIC CANE SUGAR, OR MONK FRUIT SUGAR, TO NAME A FEW!

A dried goji berry is tiny, but if you measured its nutrients, it would be the size of the moon (okay, maybe not that big, but BiG). Each bright red berry is JAM-PACKED with vitamins, minerals, antioxidants (cell protectors), and phytochemicals (plant nutrients), making gojis one of THE MOST NUTRITIOUS foods on the planet.

RED BALLOON TEA

SERVES 1

goji BERRiES

WATer

Place a BiG five-finger pinch of goji berries in a ☕. Boil a small teapot of water,

ADULT ALERT

then carefully pour it over the berries. Let the tea sit for a couple of minutes until the water turns red and the berries PLUMP up into tiny balloons. Drink HOT or COLD, and eat the gojis last.

Me, GOJI, SMALL BUT MIGHTY!

GOJI BERRIES HAVE BEEN USED IN CHINESE MEDICINE FOR THOUSANDS OF YEARS TO STRENGTHEN PEOPLE'S HEALTH AND PREVENT ILLNESS. THE BERRY IS SO NUTRITIOUS, IT HAS BEEN DECLARED A CHINESE NATIONAL TREASURE!

VERY NONDAIRY NUT MILK

MAKES 1 CUP

OR

THE FAST WAY:

BLEND, that's it! { 1 HEAPING TABLESPOON ALMOND BUTTER
1 CUP WATER }

THE LONGER BUT SMOOTHER, CREAMIER WAY:

1 CUP WATER

¼ CUP CASHEWS OR ALMONDS
(best soaked in water overnight if you can, then rinsed

A DASH OR 2 OF SALT*

A VERY LIGHT SWIRL of AGAVE*

YOU'RE NUTTY.

YOU ARE.

*This won't really make your milk taste salty or sweet, but it REALLY does improve the flavor.

Blend all ingredients in a blender on HIGH until super smooth. Now...you can drink it AS IT IS—it's most nutritious this way— but it might be a little grainy from the teeny tiny flecks of nuts. To make it smooth, pour it through a fine-mesh strainer (or nut-milk bag) into a LARGE pitcher.

NOTE: You might have to empty the strainer a couple of times if it gets clogged. Chill the milk in a sealed jar in the fridge and use within 2 or 3 days.

3 REASONS to CHOOSE NUT MILK OVER COW'S MILK

1. YOU ARE NOT A BABY COW (BUT CHECK FOR HAIRY EARS AND HOOVES JUST IN CASE).

2. MAMA COWS ARE SEPARATED FROM THEIR BABIES SO THEIR MILK CAN BE SAVED FOR HUMANS—NOT VERY NICE!

3. It TAKES 2,000 GALLONS OF WATER to PRODUCE 1 GALLON OF COW'S MILK. THAT MEANS EVERY GLASS OF COW'S MILK COSTS THE 48 GALLONS OF PRECIOUS WATER! THAT'S ENOUGH to FILL TWO BATHTUBS!

POLAR BEAR

½ CUP WATER OR COCONUT WATER

1 BANANA (FROZEN IS BEST), BROKEN UP

20 to 25 ALMONDS OR CASHEWS OR ¼ CUP ALMOND BUTTER

5 ICE CUBES

SERVES 1

Put everything in a blender. If you have a plunger for your blender, you can add more ice cubes to make it ice-creamier. Blend until smooth.

For extra nutrition, stir in some Natren nondairy probiotic powder just before you drink it—you won't taste it.

CLIMATE CHANGE IS MELTING AWAY THE POLAR BEARS' ICEY ARCTIC HABITAT, PUTTING THEM IN DANGER OF EXTINCTION—BUT OUR CHOICES CAN HELP! FARMING PLANTS INSTEAD OF ANIMALS REDUCES THE POLLUTION THAT CAUSES CLIMATE CHANGE, SO EAT YOUR VEGGIES to SAVE THE ANIMALS!

Spirulina is an algae, a water plant that makes this drink glow green. Ancient Aztec warriors ate it for strength and energy. FEEEEEL the POWER!

1 CUP COCONUT WATER

A sprinkle OR MORE OF
SPIRULINA POWDER
(BLUE-GREEN ALGAE WILL WORK, too)

Put the ingredients in a jar with a cap, then SHAKE, SHAKE, SHAKE! If you want this drink slushy and frothy, blend it in a blender with a few ice cubes.

COCOLINA

SERVES 1

LEADERS AND SCIENTISTS ARE USING SPIRULINA to SOLVE WORLD HUNGER. It TAKES little ENERGY TO GROW A LOT, it is gentle on the earth, it CLEANS THE AIR, AND it PRODUCES OXYGEN EVEN BETTER than TREES DO. IT'S ALSO BURSTING WITH VITAMINS, MINERALS, AND NUTRIENTS. TALK ABOUT A SUPERFOOD!

THE UN-STICK IN THE MUD CHOCOLATE SMOOTHIE

MAKES 1 CUP
(SERVES 1 OR 2)

Blend in a blender until smooth and creamy, using a plunger if you have one to help crush the ingredients. Taste and adjust the flavors. Blend again.

½ CUP WATER (or coconut water—in this case use fewer dates)

25 ALMONDS OR CASHEWS

2 light TEASPOONS CACAO POWDER

5 to 8 ICE CUBES (if you don't have a plunger to help crush the ice, start with 5—you can always add the other 3 after blending first)

3 DATES (NO PITS!)

A SPLASH of COCONUT OIL

OPTIONALS* (start with a sprinkle and build up to a spoonful of as many as you'd like):
SPIRULINA, CHLORELLA, BLUE-GREEN ALGAE, CHIA SEEDS, HEMP SEEDS OR POWDER, VEGAN PROTEIN POWDER, DAIRY-FREE PROBIOTIC POWDER (stir it in JUST BEFORE YOU DRINK it SO the NUTRIENTS STAY POWERFUL).

*The more optional ingredients you add, the creamier and more nutritious your smoothie will be, but you may need to add a little more water and sweetness, too...blend, taste, and decide as you go.

CACAO IS ONE OF THE MOST POWERFUL HEALTH FOODS ON THE PLANET, WITH MORE ANTIOXIDANTS (CELL PROTECTORS) THAN any OTHER FOOD and LOADS OF MAGNESIUM, A NUTRIENT THAT HELPS YOUR BODY DO OVER 300 tasks!

Have you ever met a "STICK IN THE MUD"? That is a person who would rather stick to the same old ways than discover something new. Not you and me—WE'RE UNSTUCK!

Sip this under the moonlight to calm your body before bedtime (or anytime!).

MOONBEAM TEA

SERVES 1

½ CUP WATER

½ CUP VEGAN MILK (store-bought or very NONDAIRY, page 8)

1 CHAMOMILE TEA BAG (SNiP off the tag and string)

½ teaspoon AGAVE

ADULT ALERT — Put everything in a small pot. Bring to a gentle boil, then turn off the heat. Cover and let it sit for a minute or 2. Pour or ladle into a mug and soon—ZZZZZZZZZ! OFF TO THE MOON you'll go.

BEES ARE CRAZY FOR CHAMOMILE! PLANT SOME TO MAKE YOUR YARD A SANCTUARY (SAFE PLACE) FOR BEES, WHO ARE DISAPPEARING DUE TO POLLUTION, PESTICIDES, HABITAT LOSS, AND CLIMATE CHANGE. "BEE" A FRIEND—THEY POLLINATE AT LEAST 30% OF OUR FOOD CROPS AND 90% OF WILD PLANTS!

I'M GETTING HUNGRY

CONDIMENTS, SAUCES & DIPS

These tiny seeds add a HUGE punch of flavor to soups, salads, and noodles. Many recipes in this book use them, so keep a batch on hand—they taste good sprinkled on everything.

TOASTED TIDBITS
SESAME SEEDS

MAKES 1/4 CUP

1/4 CUP RAW SESAME SEEDS (BLACK OR WHITE OR BOTH)

HAVE NEARBY:

A DRY, WIDE BOWL, LARGER THAN YOUR FRYING PAN

IS iT HOT iN HERE?

NOTE: This recipe is a game of senses! Use your sight and smell to know when the sesame seeds are done—because depending on your stove and pan, it could take 2 minutes or 6, and you don't want them to burn. KEEP WATCH—they're done when the white seeds turn toasty tan and the black ones get a little lighter.

Put the seeds in a dry, small frying pan on the stove. Turn the heat to medium-high. ADULT ALERT After a minute, use a wooden spatula to gently stir every 10 seconds or so, letting the seeds toast, but moving them so they don't stick. AS SOON as the seeds start to look and smell toasty, turn off the heat and pour them into the dry bowl so they stop cooking. Let cool completely.

Store somewhere cool (you can use a funnel to pour them into a little glass jar).

Eat this BEAUTIFUL sauce by itself, spread it onto toast or a Chapati (page 62), roll it in a lettuce leaf, scoop it onto Plentiful Lentifuls (page 75), dip veggies or crackers in it, or get fancy and eat it with vegan vanilla ice cream...RIDICULOUSLY yummy. Just be careful—beets stain!

SWEET BEET SAUCE

You're pretty!

MAKES ABOUT 1 CUP

2 to 3 MEDIUM-SIZE RED BEETS, STEMS REMOVED, WASHED REALLY WELL (or COOKED BEETS—SKIP THE BOILING)

½ CUP WALNUTS

1 TABLESPOON OLIVE OIL

1 TABLESPOON AGAVE

BEETS AND WALNUTS LOOK LIKE THE VERY BODY PART THEY HELP KEEP HEALTHY. (THIS ANCIENT IDEA IS CALLED THE "DOCTRINE OF SIGNATURES".) BEETS ARE DARK RED, LIKE BLOOD—AND THEY DO HELP KEEP BLOOD FLOWING SMOOTHLY.

Fill a very LARGE pot with enough water to fully cover the beets. Boil the beets (BIG, fast bubbles everywhere), until you can easily poke them with a fork, about 30 to 40 minutes.

Rinse the beets in a strainer under cool water, using your thumbs to easily peel away the skins. (They do NOT have to be perfect.) Cut the beets into chunks.

In a food processor or powerful blender with a plunger, blend all ingredients plus ¼ cup of water until smooth. Taste and add *more* agave if needed.

WALNUTS LOOK LIKE BRAINS—AND THEY CONTAIN HEALTHY FATS THAT HELP YOUR BRAIN GROW. YOU ARE WHAT YOU EAT!

This spread gets THICKER and MORE FLAVORFUL after it has chilled...if you can resist!

IDEA: Make it on a Sunday and eat it throughout the school week—on toast or crackers, carrot and celery sticks, Leaf Poppers (page 45), or Pipsqueaks (page 47).

CASHEW CREAM CHEESE

MAKES ABOUT 1 CUP

1 HEAPING CUP RAW CASHEWS, SOAKED IN WATER AT LEAST 2 HOURS (ALL DAY OR NIGHT IS EVEN BETTER)

5 TABLESPOONS WATER

2 TABLESPOONS LEMON JUICE (YOU CAN ALWAYS ADD MORE)

A HEAPING 1/2 TEASPOON SEA SALT

20

Rinse the soaked cashews.  Put all ingredients in a food processor—or even better, a high-speed blender WITH A PLUNGER (this makes the BEST, SMOOTHEST, CREAMIEST recipe). Blend until super, duper (I mean REALLY) velvety smooth. This might take a few long minutes, so make friends with the machine because you'll be hanging out while you turn it on, slowly turn it UP/DOWN/UP/DOWN/OFF, scrape down the sides, and repeat.

It might SEEM like you need to add more liquid at first, but keep processing for a solid few minutes before you do. If you NEED to, add a tablespoon of water at a time before blending again.

CASHEW!

BLESS YOU!

Taste and add a few more dashes of lemon juice and salt if it tastes too sweet. Blend once more and chill before serving (the flavors will mix and it will thicken it up a bit, too). Store in a sealed container in the fridge.

5-MINUTE TOMATO SAUCE

MAKES ABOUT 1/3 CUP (SERVES 1)

1 CUP SLICED-in-HALF CHERRY TOMATOES
(OR any SMALLISH KIND)

1/2 TEASPOON OLIVE OIL

1/4 TEASPOON CHOPPED GARLIC

5 TWO-FINGER PINCHES of SEA SALT

HAVE NEARBY:
2 TEASPOONS NUTRITIONAL YEAST

In a blender, blend the tomatoes on low in short spurts, just to chop them up a bit (you DO NOT want them to turn completely into liquid or pink foam!).

ADULT ALERT Pour the blended tomatoes into a small pan, adding the olive oil, garlic, and salt. Turn the heat to high. Stir and let the sauce get HOT and BUBBLY, then simmer (medium bubbles everywhere) for about 3 minutes, stirring throughout. Add the nutritional yeast and stir for another minute or so as the sauce thickens.

Turn off the heat, taste, and add more salt if needed.

Once you see how easy this recipe is, you can double or triple the measurements for larger batches to share. Mix it with pasta, kelp noodles, or grains, or use it on a Chapati Pizzati (page 63).

Each time you make this, it can be different—you might add more lemon, try a different nut, or use more basil than spinach. Eat it by the spoonful, use it as a dip, spread, or salad dressing, a spread for Chapatis (page 62) or mix it onto some pasta or kelp noodles.

PRESTO PESTO

SPINACH and BASIL

MAKES ABOUT 1 CUP

Rinse {

2 GIGANTIC as-much-as-you-can-grab handfuls OF FRESH SPINACH LEAVES
(A HEAPING 2 cups SUPER, DUPER, REALLY packed in)

1 BIG HANDFUL OF BASIL LEAVES (a HEAPING ½ cup REALLY packed in)

½ CUP CASHEWS, MACADAMIA NUTS, OR PINE NUTS

¼ CUP OLIVE OIL

¼ TEASPOON SEA SALT

LEMON JUICE (at least 1 GIANT wedge squeezed, or as much as 2 tablespoons)

½ CLOVE GARLIC (you can always add more)

24

Nuts?
NEVER SAW 'EM.

ADULT ALERT Blend in a food processor or a powerful blender (one with a plunger, which you'll need to help mix and stir while the machine is on) until the pesto is as coarse (gritty) or smooth as you want it.

Stop, taste, and adjust up to ONE MILLION times. Does it need a little salt? Add a PINCH. Want it THINNER? Add a little olive oil. THICKER? Add a few more nuts. STRONGER? Add more basil or the other half of the garlic clove. There's no right way—just the way YOU like it!

REASONS TO BUY FRESH FOOD FROM FARMERS' MARKETS:

1. OFTEN, THE MORE YOU BUY, THE BETTER THE DISCOUNT.
2. BUYING FRESH CUTS DOWN ON PLASTIC AND PACKAGING THAT WOULD END UP IN A LANDFILL OR THE OCEAN.
3. BUYING FOOD GROWN NEARBY CUTS SHIPPING FUEL.
4. FARMERS CONNECT US TO MOTHER NATURE...AND THEY'RE USUALLY FRIENDLY, TOO. ASK THEM QUESTIONS ABOUT IMPORTANT STUFF LIKE BUGS, SOIL, FOOD, AND PLANTS!

Use this thick sauce as a spread, a dip, on a bowl of pasta (mac 'n' cheese style), or with grains and beans. It's used in this book in Chapati Pizzati (page 63) and Bag of Tricks Cheezy Kale Chips (page 51).

CHEEZY SAUCE

MAKES 1 CUP

1 CUP RAW CASHEWS, soaked in water AT LEAST 2 hours or overnight

½ RED BELL PEPPER, RIPPED UP

¼ CUP NUTRITIONAL YEAST

3 TABLESPOONS WATER

1 TABLESPOON BRAGG LIQUID AMINOS ← for Bag of Tricks Cheezy Kale Chips (page 51), make that 2 tablespoons and a little more lemon juice

BIG LEMON WEDGE, SQUEEZED

10+ SHAKES TURMERIC

You DON'T need to SQUEEZE me to make something cheezy! Using nuts instead of milk to make cheese saves land, energy, water, and...me!

Rinse and drain the cashews.
Blend everything in a food processor or high-speed blender until VERY, VERY SMOOTH (this could take a few minutes).

I'M A LITTLE HUNGRY

SMALLER MEALS

BLAZE A TRAIL

Trail mix is a smart snack to bring along on hikes. It's light to carry, you don't need utensils, the sweets give you energy quickly, and the fats in the nuts and seeds make that energy last—whether you're playing at school or climbing a mountain.

Choose a recipe and mix together a HANDFUL OF EACH INGREDIENT (or make up your own combo!).

SUPERFOOD

RAW CASHEWS,
CACAO NIBS,
PUMPKIN SEEDS,
GOJI BERRIES,
DRIED COCONUT

TROPICAL VACATION

DRIED MANGO,
DRIED PINEAPPLE,
MACADAMIA NUTS,
DRIED COCONUT

ALWAYS & FOREVER

ROLLED OATS,
ALMONDS,
RAISINS,
DRIED COCONUT

MEDITERRANEAN

DRIED APRICOTS;
DRIED DATES;
DRIED FIGS;
ALMONDS, WALNUTS,
OR PISTACHIOS

YOUR BRAIN, MADE OF NEARLY 60% FAT,
ISN'T DONE FORMING WHEN YOU'RE BORN.
IT KEEPS CHANGING THROUGHOUT YOUR
LIFE, ESPECIALLY WHEN YOU'RE A KID—THAT'S
WHY IT'S IMPORTANT TO EAT **HEALTHY** FATS,
LIKE THOSE IN SEEDS AND NUTS, WHICH FEED
YOUR **EVER-GROWING** BRAIN!
HELP YOUR BRAIN, AND YOUR BRAIN WILL
HELP **YOU** MAKE WISE, HEALTHY, AND
THOUGHTFUL DECISIONS.

Bananas and apples with plain almond butter are just as good, but this mixture will **BOOST YOUR ENERGY** even higher in the sky!

POWER TOWERS

SERVES 1

Mix in a little BOWL
{
1 BANANA
1½ TABLESPOONS ALMOND BUTTER
½ TEASPOON CACAO POWDER
¼ TEASPOON AGAVE

OR

APPLE
ALMOND OR PEANUT BUTTER

Slice the banana into coins. Put a dab of the almond butter mixture onto each slice. Build towers.

Cut the apple in half and then place the flat side down to slice up the rest safely. Dab almond butter onto the apple slices and stack, or use the almond butter as a dip.

PACKING THESE IN YOUR LUNCH BOX? KEEP THE APPLES FRESH BY SQUEEZING A FEW DROPS OF LEMON OR ORANGE

THE ANTIOXIDANTS IN COLORFUL FRUITS AND VEGGIES DO THE SAME THING IN

ANTIOXIDANTS (CELL PROTECTORS), IT STOPS THE APPLES FROM TURNING BROWN ("OXIDIZING"). THE

There are TEENY, TINY, itsy, BiTSY, EENTSY, WEENtSY nutrients in yogurt called "probiotics," which help keep your belly and digestion healthy. You don't need dairy to get them—try rice, almond, or coconut yogurt instead.

PARTY iN a CUP

SERVES 1

½ CUP PLAIN OR VANiLLA VEGAN YOGURt

TOPPiNG iDEAS:

FRESH BERRIES
GOJi BERRIES
BANANA slices

ALMONDS   HEMP seeds   CACAO NiBS
PUMPKIN seeds   CHiA SEEDS   SHREDDED COCONUT
GRANOLA CRUMBLE (PAGE 38)

OPTIONAL: agave OR MAPLE SYRUP

Put the yogurt in a small bowl, then create something pretty with the toppings. (Use only what you'll REALLY eat, though!) If you'd like, add a drizzle of agave or maple syrup on top.

THE LEPRECHAUN FOOTPRINT AVO TOAST

SERVES 1

1 SLICE OF BREAD (try sprouted whole grain)

¼ to ½ AVOCADO (sliced OR mashed)

SEA SALT

SPIRULINA POWDER

Toast the bread until it is browned to your liking. Top with avocado. Sprinkle with salt and a trail of spirulina powder.

LOOK FOR BREADS, TORTILLAS, AND OTHER FOODS MADE WITH "SPROUTED" GRAINS, BEANS, OR SEEDS. THIS MEANS THAT EACH LITTLE TIDBIT SOAKED AND GREW A SPROUT BEFORE IT WAS USED. SPROUTING WAKES UP THE SLEEPING NUTRIENTS INSIDE A SEED, BEAN, OR GRAIN, WHICH COME BURSTING OUT INTO THE BEGINNINGS OF A TINY PLANT. SPROUTED FOODS CONTAIN MORE NUTRIENTS.

HOW to CUt AN AVOCADO:

1. SLiCE THE AVO tHE LONG WAY ALL aROUND.

2. TWISt ONE SIDE TOWARD YOU, THE OTHER AWAY.

3. GENtLY SQUEEZE THE PIt SIDE and the PIt WILL POP OUT.

Toast mochi and **POOF**, it BUBBLES, POPS, and PUFFS before your very eyes, becoming a chewy-on-the-inside, crispy-on-the-outside cloud. This is hilarious to watch and delicious to eat.

PUFF LOVE
MOCHI, 2 WAYS

SERVES 1

GRAINAISSANCE ORIGINAL MOCHI (or your favorite organic brand)

PICK ONE:

SWEET:
ALMOND BUTTER
JAM OR agave

SAVORY:
$\frac{1}{4}$ to $\frac{1}{2}$ AVOCADO (mashed OR sliced)
OR VEGAN CREAM CHEESE
(store-bought OR Cashew Cream Cheese, page 20)
A SPRINKLE of SEA SALT

HOTTER, HOTTER, HOTTER, KABO

OOOOOOM!

Preheat an oven or a toaster oven as the mochi package directs (usually 450°F).

ADULT ALERT

Chop a 1½-inch-wide strip off one side of a mochi block. Then cut that strip into 4 or 5 squares (save the rest of the mochi in the fridge).

Spread out the squares on a baking sheet and bake them in the oven according to the package directions (8 to 10 minutes) until the squares PUFF up and become toasty brown in spots.

Turn off the oven. Using an oven mitt, carefully remove the sheet. Break open each puff and fill it with tiny spoonfuls of sweet or savory toppings.

This sweet cereal snack is yummy by itself,
in a bowl with vegan milk, or sprinkled on vegan yogurt
or Chocolate Mousse (page 110).

GRANOLA CRUMBLE

MAKES ABOUT 1½ CUPS (SERVES 2 OR 3)

1 CUP ROLLED OATS

¼ CUP COCONUT FLAKES

20 ALMONDS

2 TABLESPOONS AGAVE
OR MAPLE SYRUP

1 teaspoon WHITE SESAME SEEDS

½ teaspoon VANILLA extract

A few HEFTY SHAKES OF CINNAMON

A SPRINKLING of RAISINS
(ADD AFTER BAKING)

Preheat the oven to 325°F. In a large bowl, mix together all ingredients
(except the raisins) until ALL the oats get sticky. Spread onto a baking
sheet, then set a timer FOR JUST 5 MINUTES. Place the sheet in the
oven, start the timer, and STAY CLOSE BY—granola is easy to burn!
While you wait, get your mitts and spatula ready.

The second the timer goes "DING!", (ADULT ALERT) use mitts to take out the baking sheet. Swish the granola around with a spatula, then place it back in the oven for another 2 minutes. Quickly remove it from the oven, stir again, and let cool completely—as it does, the oats will harden up. Sprinkle in the raisins last.

Best eaten wearing pajamas, covered in blankets, reading a book, or snuggling with a loved one (preferably someone soft and furry).

SNIFF
SNIFF
SNIFF

SNIFF
SNIFF

1 SLICE SPROUTED WHOLE GRAIN BREAD
COCONUT OIL
A LIGHT DRIZZLE AGAVE
CINNAMON

Toast the bread as light or dark as you like it. While it's still warm, spread a thin layer of coconut oil over the surface, along with a drizzle of agave. Lightly sprinkle cinnamon on top.

CINNAMON COMES FROM THE BARK OF A CINNAMON TREE. FOR THOUSANDS OF YEARS, IT HAS BEEN USED BY PEOPLE AROUND THE WORLD FOR ITS FLAVOR, AROMA, AND AS A MEDICINE TO BALANCE BLOOD SUGAR, FIGHT GERMS, AND IMPROVE DIGESTION.

COZY KITCHEN CINNAMON TOAST

SERVES 1

41

Out with the old peanut-butter-and-jelly combo,
and in with the new!

DINO ROLLS

ALMOND BUTTER

GOJI BERRIES, RAISINS, CHOPPED DATES, OR JAM

LONG STRIPS OF DINO KALE, RINSED, STEMS REMOVED

Spread some almond butter and a few gojis, raisins,
date pieces, or a little jam onto the end of a long strip of
kale. Starting on that end, roll it up, and enjoy!

TODAY, THOUSANDS OF ANIMALS ARE IN SERIOUS DANGER OF BECOMING EXTINCT (GONE, LIKE DINOSAURS!), DUE TO HUNTING, POLLUTION, AND THE DESTRUCTION OF NATURAL HABITATS. BY CHOOSING PLANT-BASED FOODS, WHICH ARE GENTLER ON THE ENVIRONMENT, YOU BECOME A **CONSERVATIONIST**, SOMEONE WHOSE CHOICES HELP PROTECT NATURE AND THE WELL-BEING OF **ALL** LIVING THINGS.

LAND & SEA CHEWS

A SMALL HANDFUL OF DRY SEAWEED
(TRY NORI/LAVER, KELP, PALM, ARAME, OR WAKAME)

A HANDFUL OF RAW CASHEWS

Rip the seaweed into bite-size pieces (or cut with a scissors). Mix with cashews for a salty, chewy, creamy combo snack.

I'LL PROTECT YOU!

I'LL PROTECT YOU!

A MINERAL CALLED IODINE IN SEAWEED HELPS PROTECT YOUR BODY FROM RADIOACTIVE POLLUTION, BASICALLY GIVING YOU SUPERHERO POWERS! EAT SEAWEED TO KEEP YOUR SUPERPOWERS STRONG.

Basil is nice for these little bites, but you can use ANY fresh herb or small-leafed greens. Try baby spinach, mint, tatsoi, arugula, chervil, or parsley.

LEAF POPPERS

LOOKS GOOD to me!

← Folivore (only eats) leaves

VEGAN CREAM CHEESE
(STORE-BOUGHT OR CASHEW CREAM CHEESE, PAGE 20) OR HUMMUS

BASIL LEAVES, RINSED

SEA SALT

Place a DAB of vegan cream cheese or hummus onto each leaf.

SPRINKLE with salt and POP it in your chops!

THROUGHOUT HISTORY, HERBS HAVE BEEN TREASURED BY HUMANS. COOKS LOVE THEIR FLAVORS AND OILS, MEDICINE-MAKERS HAVE USED THEM FOR THEIR HEALING POWERS, CEREMONY LEADERS CHERISH THEM FOR THEIR POWERFUL FRAGRANCES, AND GARDENERS USE THEM TO PROTECT THEIR OTHER PLANTS FROM INSECTS AND OTHER ANIMALS. PLANT BASIL NEAR YOUR WINDOWS TO KEEP FLIES AND MOSQUITOES AWAY!

POP

A tea sandwich is an itty-bitty sandwich served as a snack at tea time...but you can break the rules and eat them anytime.

PIPSQUEAK
TEA SANDWICHES

SERVES 1

VEGAN CREAM CHEESE (STORE-BOUGHT OR CASHEW CREAM CHEESE, PAGE 20)

2 SLICES OF WHOLE GRAIN BREAD (TRY SPROUTED)

4 OR MORE CUCUMBER SLICES

SEA SALT and BLACK PEPPER

Spread a thick layer of cream cheese onto both slices of bread. Lay the cucumbers on 1 piece of bread, add salt and pepper, then stack the second piece of bread on top. Cut the sandwich in half and then in half again to make 4 tiny sandwiches (a large flat-edge knife is best, so you can press straight down instead of sawing back and forth).

RAW FOODS CONTAIN THE MOST ENERGY AND NUTRIENTS. MAKE YOUR SANDWICH EVEN HEALTHIER BY ADDING FRESH INGREDIENTS: SPROUTS, LEAFY GREENS, HERBS, TOMATOES, AVOCADO.

LIFEBOATS

1 OR 2 BIG LEAVES OF SOFT LETTUCE

½ AVOCADO, mashed OR SLICED

SEAWEED (SHEETS CUT INTO SLIVERS, OR A CRUNCHY
KIND LIKE ARAME OR HiJiKi, OR FLAKES LIKE KELP)

SEA SALT

Lay out your lettuce. Put some avocado
on top. Sprinkle with lots of seaweed and
a little salt. Fold each lettuce leaf into a
little boat and sail it into your mouth.

NORi SEAWEED SNACKS
CUT INTO SLIVERS
PLUS ARAME

Did you know that AVOCADO is a fruit?

RAW (UNCOOKED) PLANT FOODS ARE FULL OF LIFE—WANT TO SEE? RINSE AND DRY THE AVOCADO PIT. WITH THE POINTY END FACING THE SKY, POKE 3 OR 4 TOOTHPICKS ALL AROUND THE PIT'S MIDDLE SO THE PIT CAN BE SUSPENDED IN A GLASS CUP OR JAR. FILL THE CUP WITH WATER UNTIL IT COVERS THE BOTTOM HALF OF THE PIT. PLACE IT IN A WARM PLACE OUT OF DIRECT SUNLIGHT. KEEP THE WATER LEVEL UP, AND IN 2 TO 6 WEEKS, YOUR PIT WILL BE GROWING ITS OWN AVOCADO TREE!

49

NOTE: You **MUST** have parchment or waxed paper, or this amazing oven trick won't work—the leaves will stick to the baking sheet and you'll be sad and hungry. Don't let this happen.

BAG of TRICKS CHEEZY KALE CHIPS

4 BIG KALE LEAVES

1/4 CUP CHEEZY SAUCE (PAGE 26)

A GOOD SPRINKLING of SEA SALT

OR

4 BIG KALE LEAVES

2 TABLESPOONS NUTRITIONAL YEAST

1 TEASPOON OLIVE OIL

1/2 teaspoon BRAGG LIQUID AMINOS

ADULT ALERT Preheat the oven to 400°F. (It should warm up for at least 10 minutes.)

Rinse the kale leaves, then pat them dry with a FRESHLY clean kitchen towel. Tear the leafy parts from the stems, keeping the pieces as <u>BIG</u> as you possibly can—because they're going to shrink...a lot!

Wash your hands really well. Then, in a big mixing bowl, gently massage all the ingredients together (you can lick your fingers LAST—but then wash your hands again!). Line a baking sheet with parchment paper. Spread the kale leaves FLAT on top, making sure none overlap (it's okay if they're touching, but they shouldn't lie on top of each other).

Here's the trick! TURN THE OVEN OFF, then put the kale inside, QUICKLY closing the door. Come back in 20 minutes (NO peeking, you'll let the heat out!). If it is crisp enough, eat up! Otherwise, leave any soggy ones inside the warm oven for a little longer.

ASPARAGUS SPEARS

SERVES 2 to 4

1 BUNCH ASPARAGUS (15 to 20 SPEARS), RINSED, BOTTOM INCH OR SO SNAPPED OFF

1 teaspoon OLIVE OIL

1 teaspoon BRAGG LIQUID AMINOS

A BIG LEMON WEDGE, SQUEEZED

NUTRITIONAL YEAST (this gives it a REALLY yummy cheesy taste)

OPTIONAL: A SPRINKLING OF DRIED HERBS (like an Italian Seasoning or herbes de Provence)

Preheat oven to 400°F. Lay the asparagus on a baking sheet that has a rim. Pour the liquid ingredients right on top, then push the asparagus around to make sure each one gets coated. Line up the spears and sprinkle on the nutritional yeast and herbs, if you're using them, last.

ADULT ALERT place in the oven for 10 to 12 minutes until they begin to look toasty brown in spots, then remove with mitts and spear yourself! **NOTE:** If you turn the oven off and leave them inside a little longer, they'll crisp up more—you might like them like that.

THERE ARE GOOD SPEARS (ASPARAGUS!) AND BAD SPEARS—LIKE THE KIND USED TO HUNT ELEPHANTS. EVERY YEAR, ABOUT 35,000 ELEPHANTS ARE KILLED BY ILLEGAL HUNTERS CALLED POACHERS, WHO TAKE THE IVORY TUSKS AND SELL THEM FOR DECORATION, JEWELRY, CHOPSTICKS, COMBS, AND OTHER TRINKETS. YOU CAN HELP BY RAISING MONEY FOR WILDLIFE CONSERVATION GROUPS THAT GUARD HABITATS AND BY PROMISING **NEVER** TO BUY ANYTHING MADE OF ANIMAL PARTS.

MUSHROOM JERKY

SERVES 2

2 LARGE PORTOBELLO MUSHROOMS (RINSE and SHAKE OFF WATER WELL)

OPTIONAL: KETCHUP for DIPPING

WHISK iN a BiG CUP {
- ¼ CUP WATER
- 1 TABLESPOON BRAGG LiQUID AMINOS OR SHOYU
- 2 teaspoons DiJON MUSTARD (it WON'T MAKE the 'SHROOMS SPICY)
- 1 teASPOON OLiVE OiL

Gently break off the mushroom stems and tear them in half. Slice each 'shroom cap into 6 to 8 strips about the same size, then place ALL pieces in a large baking dish that has sides. Pour the whisked sauce onto the 'shrooms, then gently PUSH, FLIP, AND RUB each piece around like a sponge to soak up as much juice as possible.

Preheat the oven to 400°F. Meanwhile, let the 'shrooms soak in the sauce (this is called "marinating") for 10 minutes. You can keep pressing them into the sauce. NOTE: If you'd rather eat juicier mushroom strips, you can skip the next baking sheet part and cook these in the soaking/baking dish for just 10 to 15 minutes.

Grease a baking sheet with a drizzle of olive oil and lay the 'shrooms on top.

Bake for 20 minutes, then (ADULT ALERT) turn off the oven and use tongs to remove any small pieces so they don't burn. Leave the rest of the 'shrooms in the still-warm oven for another 20 minutes or so (the longer you leave them in, the drier and more jerky-like they'll become, so check along the way and take them out when they're done to your liking). Dip in ketchup, if you want.

ONE WAY TO PROTECT ANIMALS IS TO CREATE NEW TRADITIONS. OVER FORTY-SIX MILLION TURKEYS ARE KILLED FOR THANKSGIVING EVERY YEAR. MOST EVERY OTHER TRADITIONAL THANKSGIVING DISH IS ALREADY PLANT-BASED—TRY A NEW CUSTOM AND MAKE THE ENTIRE MEAL ANIMAL-FREE, TOO! WHAT BETTER WAY TO CELEBRATE THANKFULNESS THAN TO SHOW RESPECT FOR ALL LIVING BEINGS?

EDIBLE FIREWORKS

POPCORN, 3 WAYS

You don't need butter to make great popcorn—olive oil does the trick and makes your toppings stick.

MAKES ABOUT 14 CUPS
(1 GIANT MIXING BOWL)

BEST EVER BASIC:
1/2 CUP ORGANIC POPCORN KERNELS
3 TABLESPOONS OLIVE OIL
1/4 TEASPOON SEA SALT

YELLOW CHEEZY:
BEST EVER BASIC
+ 2 HEAPING teaspoons NUTRITIONAL YEAST
+ A HEAPING ½ teaspoon TURMERIC

SPIRULINI GREENIE:
BEST EVER BASIC
+ 1 HEAPING teaspoon SPIRULINA POWDER

AIR-POP* the kernels into the largest mixing bowl you can find. Zigzag the olive oil on top, then add the salt plus any other toppings to make the other flavors. With clean hands, toss and mix well. Taste and adjust flavors, adding a bit more olive oil if it feels dry. NOTE: It's a scientific fact that popcorn tastes best when shared.

*IF YOU DON'T HAVE AN AIR-POPPER:

A) Sprinkle the Cheezy or Greenie toppings onto your favorite store-bought popped popcorn.

— OR —

B) Get an adult to pop the corn on the stovetop. Grease the bottom of a very large pot with a little olive oil. Add the kernels and cover. Turn heat to high. Using mitts, gently shimmy and shake the pot side to side over the flame so the pot doesn't burn. Let out a little air from time to time, cover again, and keep shaking. Soon you'll hear POP! POP! POP! Keep shimmying and shaking with the cover on. It's ready when the popping slows or stops (after about 2 to 3 minutes of popping).

ADULT ALERT

WHEN YOU FIND A VEGAN TREAT YOU LOVE, SHARE IT! TAKE IT TO SCHOOL, MAKE IT WITH A FRIEND, OR TAKE IT TO A PARTY.

57

MONKEY BUSINESS

SERVES 1

1 BANANA

COCONUT OIL

A SPRINKLE OF HEMP SEEDS

Peel the banana, then slice it down its center (the long way) or into bite-size pieces. Spread a very tiny bit of coconut oil on top and sprinkle with hemp seeds.

For school: Pack an UNPEELED banana and a small container of hemp seeds mixed with a few drops of coconut oil. Peel and dip at recess.

HEMP SEEDS CONTAIN A VERY HEALTHY FAT CALLED OMEGA-3. OUR BODIES TURN SHORT PIECES OF OMEGA-3 INTO LONG ONES THAT ACTUALLY FORM PARTS OF OUR BRAIN! EATING COCONUT OIL WITH HEMP SEEDS HELPS YOUR BODY DO THIS JOB TWO TIMES BETTER!

Soaking ingredients together ("MARINATING") can make a tasty dish EVEN MORE FLAVORFUL. Prepare these ingredients and let them have a slumber party in the fridge overnight (or AT LEAST 15 MINUTES if you can't wait!).

BROCCOLI BASH

MAKES 2 CUPS (SERVES 2 or 3)

RINSE {

1 MEDIUM CROWN of BROCCOLI (about as wide as your hand spread out), broken into very small trees with short trunks (2 to 2½ cups)

1 CARROT, GRATED

1 LEAF PURPLE CABBAGE, CHOPPED SMALL (fold it up, then slice or snip)

1 teaspoon TOASTED TIDBITS (Page 16)

OPTIONAL: FRESH GINGER, GRATED OR CHOPPED SMALL

DRESSING:
1 TABLESPOON OLIVE OIL
2 teaspoons BRAGG LIQUID AMINOS
2 teaspoons WATER

Combine all ingredients in a large, very sturdy mixing bowl. MIX AND MASH with a sturdy wooden spoon until your arm is tired. Then DO IT SOME MORE. Switch hands, and DO IT EVEN MORE! Go for at least 5 whole minutes or more, until the broccoli breaks up, shrinks down, and softens up. The more you MIX, MASH, AND BASH, the softer the broccoli becomes. Let it sit for at least 15 minutes, or, leave it in a sealed container in the fridge overnight. Taste and add a little more Bragg's and/or olive oil if needed.

Smash!

Mash!

Bash!

ONE OF THE STRONGEST, FIERCEST, MOST DANGEROUS ANIMALS IN THE WORLD IS THE HIPPOPOTAMUS—AND IT only EATS PLANTS!

"Chapati" is a word from India for "round flatbread"—like a tortilla made from whole wheat. We like to use Ezekiel 4:9 Sprouted Grain Tortillas. Make them crisp in a toaster or toaster oven, OR get an adult to toast the chapati over a stovetop flame (this is the quickest):

ADULT ALERT

Turn the flame to medium, place the chapati on the burner, and shift it side to side over the fire. Flip and repeat until lightly browned in spots—usually less than a minute!

CHAPATI, 3 WAYS

SERVES 1

1 SPROUTED GRAIN TORTILLA

½ AVOCADO and/or SOME HUMMUS

A SPRINKLING of NUTRITIONAL YEAST and/or SPIRULINA

A DRIZZLE of OLIVE OIL

SEA SALT

OPTIONAL: LETTUCE, KALE, SPROUTS, PARSLEY, or FRESH BASIL

Toast the tortilla. Spread avocado and/or hummus onto half the chapati and sprinkle with the other ingredients. Fold the chapati in half or roll it up.

CHAPATI NORMATI:

1 SPROUTED GRAIN TORTILLA

ALMOND BUTTER

AGAVE, JAM, SWEET BEET SAUCE (PAGE 18), OR MAPLE SYRUP

CINNAMON

Toast the tortilla, then spread on some almond butter and a sweet topping of your choice. Lightly sprinkle with cinnamon. Roll or fold in half.

CHAPATI SWEETATI:

¼ CUP SAUCE (store-bought or 5-Minute Tomato Sauce, page 22; Tomato Tornado, page 81; or Cheezy Sauce, page 26)

1 SPROUTED GRAIN TORTILLA

2 TEASPOONS OR MORE NUTRITIONAL YEAST

SEA SALT

OPTIONAL: TOMATOES, OLIVES, BASIL, AVOCADO SLICES, PRESTO PESTO (PAGE 24)

OLIVE OIL

CHAPATI PIZZATI:

Preheat a toaster oven to 350°F. Spread sauce on the entire surface of the tortilla. Sprinkle nutritional yeast and salt (plus tomatoes, olives, or presto pesto, if using) on top. Toast for 5 to 8 minutes, or until the edges begin to brown. Carefully remove (HOT!) and drizzle with a little olive oil. Add any basil or avocado last, if using.

63

Hungry Caterpillar
Nori Rolls

SERVES 1

½ AVOCADO OR MORE, SLICED OR MASHED
1 NORI SHEET
FILLING OPTIONS (any or all!):
CUCUMBER CUT INTO STRIPS, BITS OF GREEN ONION,
TOASTED TIDBITS (VERY YUMMY, PAGE 16), GRATED CARROT, SPROUTS
(RINSE WELL!), SPINACH, OR any SOFT LEAFY GREENS

BRAGG LIQUID AMINOS OR SHOYU to DIP

Lay the avocado in a strip along one end of a nori sheet. Neatly line up
any other filling ingredients on top of or alongside the avo. Starting with
the veggie end, roll the nori sheet into a tube as tight as you
can. Dip each bite into a little pool of Bragg's or shoyu.

NOTE: For picnics or school lunches,
use 2 sheets of nori instead of 1. It
will keep your rolls from getting soggy.

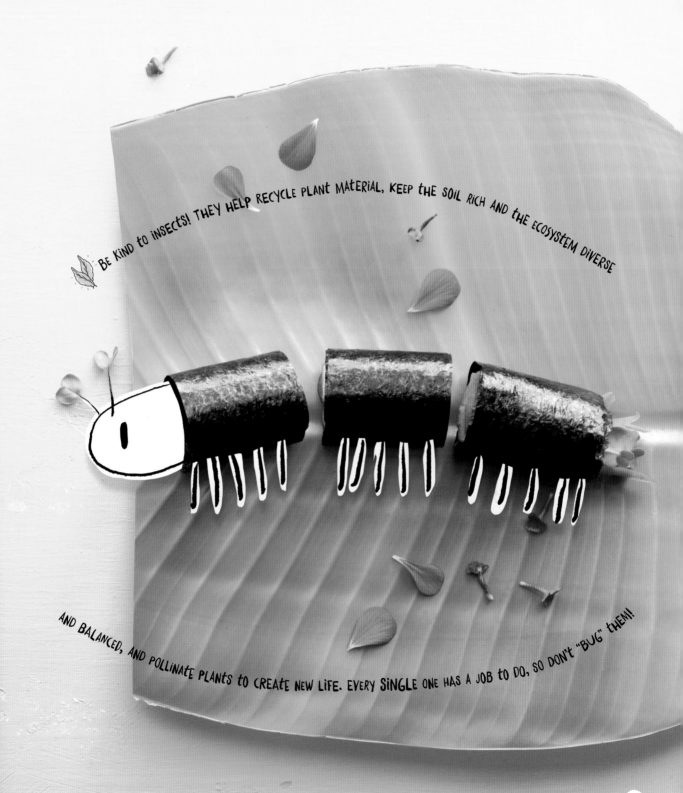

BE KIND TO INSECTS! THEY HELP RECYCLE PLANT MATERIAL, KEEP THE SOIL RICH AND THE ECOSYSTEM DIVERSE

AND BALANCED, AND POLLINATE PLANTS TO CREATE NEW LIFE. EVERY SINGLE ONE HAS A JOB TO DO, SO DON'T "BUG" THEM!

OODLES OF NOODLES

SESAME SOBA

SERVES 4

Have an adult cook these; you do the rest.

1 (8-OUNCE) PACKAGE SOBA NOODLES

1 GREEN ONION, CHOPPED

1 TABLESPOON TOASTED TIDBITS*
(PAGE 16)

2 TABLESPOONS BRAGG LIQUID AMINOS

2 TEASPOONS OLIVE OIL

OPTIONAL: FRESH GINGER,
GRATED OR CHOPPED SMALL

ADULT ALERT Cook the soba noodles according to the package directions, then rinse and drain off as much water as possible. Put the noodles in a large mixing bowl, then add the rest of the ingredients. Stir gently. Serve warm, or chill in the fridge.

*Don't skip these, they are the stars of this show!

BY CHOOSING ORGANIC INGREDIENTS (FOODS GROWN WITHOUT CHEMICALS), WE PROTECT RIVERS, LAKES, AND SWAMPS FROM TOXINS THAT WOULD HARM THE PLANTS, INSECTS, FISH, AND BIRDS THAT ARE PART OF THOSE ECOSYSTEMS. LITTLE CHOICES HAVE BIG IMPACTS!

Couscous is basically magical. One minute, it's a tiny hard speck; five minutes later, it's BIG, soft, and fluffy! And in this recipe you "dye" it pink! The pistachios add beautiful colors, too. This is so easy to make, you'll be tickled pink.

½ CUP WHOLE WHEAT COUSCOUS

2 THICK SLICES RED BEET ← Watch out, they stain!

3-INCH PIECE OF GREEN ONION, CHOPPED

OPTIONAL: 15 to 20 PISTACHIOS

1 TEASPOON OLIVE OIL

1 LIGHT TEASPOON DRIED HERB MIX
(like Italian seasoning or herbes de Provence)

A LIGHT ¼ TEASPOON SEA SALT
(you can always add MORE)

HAVE NEARBY: A SMALL EMPTY BOWL AND SOME TONGS

Measure the couscous and set it aside. Put the beets in a small pot with ¾ cup water. **ADULT ALERT** Bring the water to a BIG boil, then turn off the heat. QUICKLY, use tongs to remove the beets and save them in the little bowl (you'll use them again), then pour the couscous into the pot of BEET-RED water, gently shimmying the pot to distribute it evenly. Cover the pot and let it sit for 5 whole minutes (NO PEEKING!).

READY FOR MAGIC? Lift the lid and...POOF! Gently fluff the puffy couscous with a fork, then tumble it into a medium bowl and add the rest of the ingredients. To make it even pinker, chop up the beet slices and add them, too, along with any drops of beet juice from the little bowl. Stir to spread the color. Taste and add salt or more herbs if needed. Eat warm or cold.

MANY COMPANIES ADD CHEMICAL COLORS TO JUNK FOOD TO GET YOUR ATTENTION—THEY'RE TRYING TO DO WHAT NATURE HAS ALREADY DONE! THE HEALTHIEST FOODS ARE COLORFUL AND EYE-CATCHING—NATURALLY!

PINK COUSCOUS

MAKES 2 CUPS (SERVES 2)

EVEN MORE COLORFUL WITH A SCOOP OF PRESTO PESTO (PAGE 24) OR SWEET BEET SAUCE (PAGE 18)!

Tempeh is just soybeans or grains formed into a block. In this recipe, it tastes similar to tuna salad—but the fish get to stay in the sea.

PRETEND TUNA SALAD

MAKES 2 CUPS (SERVES 3 OR 4)

8-OUNCE PACKAGE TEMPEH (TRY LIGHTLIFE'S ORIGINAL OR 3-GRAIN)

1 BIG STALK CELERY, SLICED THE LONG WAY AND THEN CHOPPED SMALL

1/4 CUP + 1 TABLESPOON VEGENAISE

A few BIG SLIVERS OF RED ONION, CHOPPED (ABOUT 1 HEAPING TABLESPOON)

A SMALL HANDFUL OF PARSLEY LEAVES (ABOUT 1/4 CUP)

1/4 TEASPOON SEA SALT

BLACK PEPPER

TODAY, MORE THAN 70% OF THE WORLD'S FISH, INCLUDING ALL TUNA, ARE QUICKLY NEARING EXTINCTION, DUE TO FISHING, POLLUTION, HABITAT DESTRUCTION, AND CLIMATE CHANGE. SOME SCIENTISTS SAY THAT IF WE DON'T HELP, THE OCEAN WILL BE EMPTY IN THE NEXT 30 TO 40 YEARS. IT'S TIME TO GET SERIOUS ABOUT SAVING THE FISH!

Chop the tempeh—like a tic-tac-toe grid but with many more lines—into small chunks and crumbles. Put it in a steamer basket and place the basket inside a pot filled with about 1 inch of water. **ADULT ALERT** Bring to a **BiG** boil, then turn the heat to medium and cover. Steam for 10 minutes until the tempeh is soft to chew. Remove the lid and let it cool COMPLETELY.

Mix and mash all the ingredients in a large bowl to break up the tempeh more. This recipe tastes best if you let the flavors soak in (it really makes a difference!), so try chilling it in the fridge for an hour or even overnight…if you can resist.

4 WAYS TO ENJOY:

1. By itself with crackers, celery sticks, or sauerkraut.
2. Rolled in a tortilla or a sheet of nori seaweed.
3. On a sandwich or rice cracker (try adding pickles, lettuce, tomato, mustard).
4. Rolled in lettuce or cabbage leaves.

Thank you!

After you make this recipe once, you'll hardly need the measurements again, no matter how much quinoa you cook. A sprinkle of this, a few shakes of that—and done!
NOTE: Leftovers are BRIGHTER yellow and EVEN TASTIER!

COLORFUL FOODS LIKE TURMERIC ARE VERY POWERFUL! FOR CENTURIES, TURMERIC HAS BEEN USED FOR FLAVOR AND AS AN ANTI-INFLAMMATORY MEDICINE TO FIGHT GERMS AND HEAL PAIN, BRUISES, AND SWELLING.

GOLDEN QUINOA

MAKES 3 CUPS (SERVES 2 to 4)

3 CUPS COOKED QUINOA (directions below)

2 to 3 TABLESPOONS RAISINS (golden looks best)

I like to chop or snip them up with clean scissors

A SMALL HANDFUL of PARSLEY LEAVES, CHOPPED

A HEAPING 1/4 teaspoon TURMERIC

OPTIONAL: A LOOSE 1/8 teaspoon CHOPPED GARLIC (teeny tiny bits)

DRESSING {
2 teaspoons OLIVE OIL
1 1/4 teaspoons BRAGG LIQUID AMINOS
A FEW BIG PINCHES of SALT
}

Let the cooked quinoa cool some, then mix **ALL** ingredients in a large bowl. The more you mix, the **BRIGHTER** the yellow becomes! **NOTE:** The turmeric can taste a bit strong at first, but let the quinoa sit for awhile, or even overnight, and the flavors will settle really nicely. Taste and add more raisins or salt if needed.

HOW to COOK QUINOA (PERFECTLY):
MAKES 3 CUPS (SERVES 2 to 4)

1 CUP QUINOA   1 1/3 CUP WATER

In a fine-mesh strainer, rinse and scrub the quinoa between your fingers until the water runs clear. Dump the quinoa in a medium pot with 1 1/3 cups of water. **(ADULT ALERT)** Bring to a boil, then cover and simmer on low (small bubbles everywhere) for 10 minutes. Turn off the heat—BUT IT'S NOT DONE YET! Fluff with a fork, then let it sit, covered, for 5 minutes or more. The edges of each grain will stay white, but any little uncooked white dots in the centers will be steamed away to fluffy perfection.

Black lentils look like teeny, tiny, shiny jewels. (NOTE: It is VERY FUN to put your hand in a bowl of dry lentils before they're cooked.) Unlike other lentils, they don't turn to mush when you cook them, so they're good to eat in a salad or on their own. Save some for tomorrow, this recipe is even better the next day.

PLENTIFUL LENTIFULS

MAKES 2 CUPS (SERVES 3 or 4)

1 CUP DRY BLACK LENTILS

A SMALL HANDFUL of PARSLEY LEAVES, CHOPPED OR RIPPED SMALL

1 TABLESPOON RED ONION, CHOPPED SMALL

TOPPING: NUTRITIONAL YEAST

DRESSING:

1 TABLESPOON DIJON MUSTARD
2 TEASPOONS AGAVE OR MAPLE SYRUP
1 TEASPOON OLIVE OIL
A HEAPING 1/4 TEASPOON SEA SALT

CASHEW CREAM CHEESE (PAGE 20)

Rinse the lentils in a fine-mesh strainer, then put them in a medium pot with 3 cups of water.

 Bring to a boil, then simmer on medium, covered, for about 15 minutes, or until the lentils are soft but not mushy (use a fork to scoop out a few and taste test). Pour the lentils into a fine-mesh strainer and rinse under cool water.

Drain, drain, drain off as much water as you can. Then, being very careful not to mash the lentils, stir all ingredients together in a large bowl. Taste and add more salt, agave, or Dijon if you wish. Sprinkle with nutritional yeast before eating.

AWESOME BLOSSOMS

SERVES 2 to 4

ADULT ALERT — HAVE AN ADULT HELP YOU CHOP EACH ONE IN HALF (FROM THE tip to the stem), THEN RINSE.

2 LARGE ARTICHOKES

SAUCE:

MAKES ½ CUP (¼ CUP PER ARTICHOKE)

½ CUP OLIVE OIL

1 to 2 TABLESPOONS LEMON JUICE (start with 1, see how you like it)

1 SMALL CLOVE GARLIC (OR a BIG one cut in half)

¼ teaspoon SEA SALT

A BIG SPLASH OF BRAGG LIQUID AMINOS

OPTIONAL: A FEW PINCHES OF a DRIED HERB MIX

Blend in a Blender until creamy, then taste. If it's too strong, add a teaspoon or 2 of water; if it's not strong enough, add more lemon, garlic, or a little more saltiness. Blend again, then divide into little bowls to share.

Place the 'chokes in a huge pot, then add water until they're fully covered. Bring to a `BIG` boil, then let it bubble on medium-high, covered, for about 40 to 45 minutes or until you can very easily pull a leaf from the middle of an artichoke. (HOT! USE TONGS!) Turn off the heat and use tongs to lift the artichokes, gently shaking off the water.

Before you chow down, spoon out the hairy, spiky pointies from the center of each artichoke. The rest of the soft center is good to eat—it's called the artichoke's heart.

Peel off a leaf, dip it in the sauce, and scrape off the soft "meat" with your teeth, tossing the rest of the leaf away. Be sure to have napkins! If you don't have sauce dribbling down your chin, you're doing it wrong. Use any leftover sauce as salad dressing.

actually
a FLOWER!

Have an adult cook a pot of plain quinoa (page 73), then use a cup at a time to make your own meal—perfect for school lunches (AND you'll have plain quinoa left over to try a new recipe tomorrow).

QUINOA
'ROUND THE WORLD
EACH RECIPE SERVES 1

QUINOA EVERYWHERE:

MIX {
1 CUP COOKED QUINOA

A SMALL HANDFUL OF CHOPPED KALE OR PARSLEY, OR a 1-INCH PIECE OF GREEN ONION, CHOPPED SMALL

1 teaspoon OLIVE OIL

¾ teaspoon BRAGG LIQUID AMINOS

SEA SALT

OPTIONAL: A SPRINKLING OF NUTRITIONAL YEAST and SPIRULINA, CHOPPED CELERY OR CARROTS, CHERRY TOMATOES, a few grains of CHOPPED RED ONION OR GARLIC

WILL MAKE YOUR QUINOA green!

QUINOA MIDDLE EARTH:

MIX

1 CUP COOKED QUINOA

A SMALL HANDFUL of CHOPPED PARSLEY OR MINT (OR BOTH!)

2 CUCUMBER SLICES, CHOPPED

A FEW CHERRY TOMATOES, CUT IN HALF

1 teaspoon OLIVE OIL

SEA SALT

OPTIONAL: BLACK PEPPER, a few CHOPPED OLIVES, LEMON JUICE

QUINOA MEX:

mix {
1 CUP COOKED QUINOA

A FEW BIG SPOONFULS COOKED BEANS
(TRY BLACK, PINTO, OR GARBANZO)

1 teaspoon OLIVE OIL

A SPRINKLING OF CILANTRO OR GREEN ONION

5 to 10 SHAKES OF CUMIN POWDER

SEA SALT
}

OPTIONAL: CHEEZY SAUCE (page 26), SALSA, A FEW CHERRY TOMATOES
CUT IN HALF, AVOCADO SLICES, BITS OF RED ONION OR GARLIC

EVERY YEAR, A GIANT PORTION OF THE WORLD'S GRAIN IS USED TO FEED SIXTY-FIVE BILLION ANIMALS RAISED FOR MEAT AND DAIRY, INSTEAD OF THE ONE BILLION PEOPLE IN THE WORLD WHO ARE HUNGRY. THE MORE PEOPLE CHOOSE TO EAT PLANT-BASED FOODS RATHER THAN ANIMALS, THE MORE GRAIN COULD BE SHARED WITH FAMILIES EVERYWHERE.

QUINOA JAPANESE:

1 CUP COOKED QUINOA

1 to 2-INCH PIECE OF GREEN ONION, CUT SMALL

1 teaspoon OLIVE OIL

3/4 TEASPOON BRAGG LIQUID AMINOS (YOU CAN ALWAYS
ADD MORE LATER, OR A DASH OF SALT, TOO. TASTE AND SEE!)

1/4 TEASPOON OR MORE TOASTED TIDBITS (PAGE 16)

add right before you eat {
A FEW AVOCADO SLICES

ROASTED SEAWEED SHEETS,
CRUMBLED, OR A 2-INCH SQUARE PIECE OF
NORI (ROLL INTO A TIGHT TUBE AND
USE CLEAN SCISSORS TO SNIP THIN STRIPS OFF
THE END—THEY'LL UNCURL INTO RIBBONS!)

This recipe is best in the summertime, when tomatoes are the biggest, sweetest, and juiciest. Then you'll have the most varieties and colors to choose from. Try them all!

YOU KNOW WHAT'S RIDICULOUSLY YUMMY ON THIS SOUP? A LITTLE DOLLOP OF CASHEW CREAM CHEESE (PAGE 20). YOU COULD ALSO USE SOUP LEFTOVERS AS A SAUCE FOR CHAPATI PIZZATI (PAGE 63).

TOMATO TORNADO

MAKES ABOUT 4 CUPS

4 to 6 GIANT tomatoes *like an adult fist, chopped into large chunks*

1 ONION, CHOPPED BIG

2 RAPUNZEL VEGETABLE BOUILLON* CUBES
with HERBS or SEA SALT

2 CUPS WATER

ADULT ALERT

Put all ingredients in a big pot. Bring to a boil (BIG, fast bubbles), then stir REALLY well to mix everything up. Turn heat to low and simmer (small, slower bubbles) for 10 to 15 minutes with the pot's lid tilted. Turn off the heat and let cool.

Once the soup is cool, scoop it into a blender. Blend <u>until smooth</u>, adding a little water if it's too thick. Reheat in the big pot.

ONE ACRE OF LAND CAN PRODUCE 50,000 POUNDS OF TOMATOES, BUT ONLY 250 POUNDS OF MEAT!

*See bouillon in Meet Some Ingredients, page viii.

This soup is so yummy, even people who normally don't like broccoli are surprised by how much they love it! You'll blend this soup at the end, so don't worry about chopping the broccoli or onion very small. Big chunks are just fine.

BROC-O-TREE BISQUE

MAKES 4½ to 5 CUPS

2 MEDIUM CROWNS BROCCOLI } About as BIG as your hand curled over each one's top (around 4 packed cups), rinsed and broken into trees with tall trunks

1 YELLOW ONION, CHOPPED

2 RAPUNZEL VEGETABLE BOUILLON* CUBES WITH HERBS OR SEA SALT

4 CUPS WATER

OPTIONAL: A BIG HANDFUL OF CASHEWS

Put everything but the cashews (if using) in a big pot. **ADULT ALERT** Bring to a boil, stir well, then cover with the lid tilted. Simmer on medium-low for 10 to 12 minutes until you can EASILY poke the trunks with a fork. Turn off the heat and remove the cover.

Once the pot cools, carefully empty it into a blender (in batches if necessary) and add the cashews. Blend well until smooth, then reheat in the big pot, stirring in some water if the soup is too thick.

*See bouillon in Meet Some Ingredients, page viii.

82

83

Rinse the lentils really well in a fine-mesh strainer, then place all ingredients in a large pot. (ADULT ALERT) Bring to a `BIG,` bubbly boil for a minute or so. Turn heat to medium-low, stir, and simmer (small bubbles all over), covered, for about 15 minutes until the lentils become very soft and mashy (stir halfway through). Turn off the heat, then stir and mash really well with a wooden spoon.

YOU HAVE OPTIONS, DEPENDING ON HOW YOU LIKE YOUR TEXTURE:

1. Enjoy it as a stew—thick and hearty. Add a few drops of olive oil to each bowl!
2. Make it thinner by stirring in 1 cup of water. Add a little salt and reheat if needed.
3. Make it perfectly smooth: First, let it cool completely, then scoop it into a blender and blend on low, adding some water if it's too thick. Reheat in the pot.

No matter how you make it, save some for tomorrow—leftovers are EVEN TASTIER after the flavors have set. NOTE: The soup will thicken overnight. Just add a little water when you reheat.

CUTTING AN ONION RELEASES SULFUR FUMES INTO THE AIR. SULFUR IS A MINERAL WHOSE SMELL IS SO STRONG IT CAN MAKE YOUR EYES WATER—BUT IT'S THIS VERY POWER THAT GOES INSIDE YOUR BODY AND STRENGTHENS YOUR SKIN, HAIR, AND NAILS, AND PROTECTS YOUR CELLS FROM DISEASE! HERE'S A TRICK: WEAR SWIM GOGGLES WHEN YOU'RE CUTTING ONIONS, AND YOU'LL BE TEAR-FREE.

*See bouillon in Meet Some Ingredients, page viii.

If you put enough love into this soup, the lentils will magically change color...they go into the pot pink and come out golden yellow! Use your mind power—I know you can do it.

LENTIL MENTAL Magic SOUP

MAKES 5 to 6 CUPS (SERVES 4 to 6)

1½ CUPS RED LENTILS

1 YELLOW ONION, CHOPPED
They can be big chunks if you're definitely going to blend the soup (see option #3); otherwise aim small

2 RAPUNZEL VEGETABLE BOUILLON* CUBES WITH HERBS OR SEA SALT

4 CUPS WATER

YAM BAMS!

with AVO BUTTER

SERVES 1

1 PURPLE, WHITE, OR ORANGE YAM, RINSED

¼ AVOCADO, MASHED

SEA SALT

OPTIONAL TOPPINGS: A DRIZZLE OF OLIVE OIL, BITS OF CHIVES, OR GREEN ONIONS

Preheat the oven or toaster oven to 400°F.

Use a fork to poke holes all over the yam—at least 10 times. This lets the steam escape while it cooks. Put the yam in a baking dish or on a baking sheet (because it might ooze a little) and bake for about 40 minutes until ADULT ALERT you can EASILY poke through the skin with a fork. If the yam is giant or you're using a big oven, it might take a bit longer. Keep watch. Use tongs to carefully remove the hot yam from the oven, then cut a slit down the middle. Spoon in the avocado. Sprinkle with salt and any toppings, if using.

I'M GREEN
SALADS* & DRESSINGS

* A salad spinner is a great kitchen tool to wash and store big batches of greens so they're easily ready to eat at any time. Chop or rip up your greens, wash and dry them in the spinner, and you can store the spinner in the fridge for days, pulling out a handful of greens whenever you please.

THE RaBBiT'S HaBiT

ROMAINE LEAVES, WASHED (SHAKE OFF WATER) OR SPIN DRY

SALAD DRESSING #1 OR #2

Break up the lettuce and drizzle with dressing or eat the leaves whole, using the dressing as a dip.

#1 SWEET & SAVORY

MAKES JUST OVER ½ CUP
(ABOUT 4 SERVINGS)

3 TABLESPOONS WATER
2 TABLESPOONS BRAGG
LIQUID AMINOS or SHOYU
2 TABLESPOONS TAHINI
2 TABLESPOONS AGAVE
} BLEND in a BLENDER

#2 CREAMY TAHINI

MAKES ALMOST 1 CUP
(a SMALL JAR, ABOUT
6 to 8 SERVINGS)

BLEND
in a BLENDER
until CREAMY
{
½ CUP WATER
¼ CUP + 1 TABLESPOON TAHINI
2 TABLESPOONS NUTRITIONAL YEAST
LEMON WEDGE, SQUEEZED
¼ teaspoon SALT
A BIG SPLASH of BRAGG LIQUID AMINOS

THE CROWD PLEASER
KALE SALAD SERVES 1

1 PACKED CUP
CLEAN PIECES KALE
(ABOUT 1 GIANT HANDFUL)

A FEW SMALL SLIVERS OF RED ONION,
CHOPPED (ABOUT A HEAPING 1/4 teaspoON)

2 TEASPOONS OLIVE OIL

1/2 TEASPOON BRAGG LIQUID AMINOS

TOPPINGS:

1 HEAPING teaspoON NUTRITIONAL YEAST

OPTIONAL: A LIGHT SPRINKLE OF SPIRULINA

NOTE: Make this salad into a bigger full-belly meal by adding hummus or garbanzo beans, cherry tomatoes, a scoop of sauerkraut, or avocado! Add more dressing and toppings if needed.

Place everything but the toppings in a medium bowl. MASH AND STIR with a wooden spoon, or with clean hands, massage the kale until it gets soft. Then add the toppings and stir more. Taste. Does it need more of anything?

HOW to REMOVE KALE STEMS:

1. WITH ONE HAND, HOLD A KALE LEAF UPSIDE DOWN BY the VERY END OF the STEM.

2. JUST BELOW that, WRAP YOUR **OTHER** HAND'S THUMB AND POINTER FINGER AROUND the **TOP** OF the STEM, THEN SLIDE **that** HAND **DOWN** to STRIP the LEAVES FROM the STEM.

CHOP OR RIP UP THE KALE LEAVES AS SMALL AS YOU'D LIKE, THEN WASH WELL IN A STRAINER OR SALAD SPINNER. SPIN, PAT DRY WITH A CLEAN TOWEL, OR SHAKE OFF the WATER (THE DRIER THE KALE, THE BETTER THE SALAD DRESSING WILL STICK).

HOW to CUT KALE into RiBBONS:

1.

2.

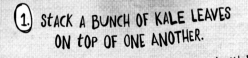

1. STACK A BUNCH OF KALE LEAVES ON TOP OF ONE ANOTHER.

2. ROLL THE STACK INTO A TUBE. CHOP THIN PIECES OFF THE END OF THE TUBE—THEY'LL UNRAVEL INTO RiBBONS!

SESAME LEMONY KALE SALAD

SERVES 1

1 PACKED CUP CLEAN
PIECES KALE
(about 1 GIANT HANDFUL)

2 TEASPOONS OLIVE OIL

½ TEASPOON BRAGG
LIQUID AMINOS

A FEW DROPS LEMON JUICE
(or up to ½ teaspoon if you like it REALLY lemony)

A HEAPING ¼ TEASPOON OR MORE
TOASTED TIDBITS (PAGE 16)

Put everything in a LARGE bowl. MASH AND STIR with a wooden spoon.

KALE VS. COW: PER CALORIE (THE UNIT OF ENERGY THAT FOOD GIVES US), KALE HAS **MORE IRON THAN BEEF** AND **MORE USABLE CALCIUM THAN MILK!** It's ALSO GENTLER ON THE EARTH TO GROW. TO PRODUCE 1 POUND OF BEEF, IT TAKES 16 POUNDS OF GRAIN, MORE THAN 2,400 GALLONS OF WATER, AND 11 TIMES MORE FOSSIL FUEL THAN KALE.

TIGER STRIPES SEAWEED SALAD

MAKES 1 HEAPING CUP (SERVES 1 or 2)

1 CUP DRY HIJIKI OR ARAME SEAWEED (about 2 handfuls)

½ CARROT, GRATED   2 teaspoons *or more* TOASTED TIDBITS (PAGE 16)

3-INCH PIECE OF GREEN ONION, CHOPPED

¼ CUP SWEET & SAVORY DRESSING (PAGE 89)

Soak the seaweed in a **BiG** bowl full of cool water for 15 minutes (it will double in size!). Then rinse in a fine-mesh strainer under cold water. Drip and shake off AS MUCH WATER AS YOU CAN (you can even squeeze the seaweed dry or pat it dry with a clean paper towel), then mix all ingredients in a big bowl along with the dressing. Let the salad chill and soak in the fridge for 10 minutes or longer.

AROUND THE WORLD, TIGERS, ORANGUTANS, ELEPHANTS, AND MANY OTHER JUNGLE SPECIES ARE LOSING THEIR HABITATS TO DEFORESTATION BY FARMS THAT PRODUCE PALM OIL, WOOD, AND PAPER. WHEN SHOPPING, LOOK FOR LABELS WITH WORDS LIKE "RECYCLED" OR "CERTIFIED SUSTAINABLE." THIS MEANS THE FARMS ARE PRACTICING WAYS OF PROTECTING ANIMALS AND THE ENVIRONMENT.

This salad is really just
guacamole and greens all mashed up!
Take the basic recipe and play with different
combinations to make it your own.

JUNGLE MASH

SERVES 1

GUACAMOLE {
1 AVOCADO
1 teaspoon or more LEMON or LIME juice
A SPRINKLE of CHOPPED red ONION or GARLIC
SEA SALT
OPTIONAL: A SPRINKLE of SPIRULINA POWDER
(to make it EXTRA GREEN and NUTRITIOUS)

ADD LAST (PICK ONE OR MIX and MATCH) {
Bits of clean LettUCE, KALE,
Basil, PARSLEY, CILANTRO, ARUGULA,
SPINACH, TATSOI, or ANY OtHeR
GREENS, BiG OR small; OLIVE OIL (IF NEEDED)

In a big, sturdy bowl, use a fork to mash together
the guacamole first. Then add the greens and STIR,
STIR, STIR! Taste and adjust the flavors. If the greens
feel a little dry, add a splash of olive oil.

ANIMAL FARMING IS ONE OF THE WORLD'S LEADING CAUSES OF DEFORESTATION. TODAY, RAIN FORESTS COVER LESS THAN 6% OF THE EARTH'S SURFACE, BUT THEY ARE STILL HOME TO MORE THAN HALF OF **ALL** THE PLANT AND ANIMAL SPECIES IN THE WORLD! TO SAVE WHAT'S LEFT, PEOPLE ARE COMING TOGETHER TO STOP DEFORESTATION AND REGROW NEW FORESTS. YOUR CLASSROOM CAN HELP BY JOINING OR RAISING MONEY FOR A CONSERVATION GROUP OR REFORESTATION PROJECT (THERE ARE **MILLIONS** OF TREES TO PLANT!).

SWEET & SOUR CUCUMBER SALAD

SERVES 1

½ MEDIUM CUCUMBER, SLICED into THIN COINS

TOASTED TIDBITS (PAGE 16)

SWEET & SOUR DRESSING:

1 TABLESPOON APPLE CIDER VINEGAR

1 TABLESPOON AGAVE

Wash your hands and nails really well. In a medium bowl, stir the dressing with your pointer finger until the agave melts in. Add the cucumbers and stir, then sprinkle with sesame seeds. Enjoy right away or put the salad in the fridge overnight to soak up the flavors even more.

This dressing is REALLY good with all soft leafy lettuces, too. To make a bigger batch for a salad, just use equal amounts of apple cider vinegar and agave.

CUCUMBER is actually a FRUIT!

I'M SWEET

DESSERTS

STRAWBERRY MOPS

SERVES 1

1 HEAPING TABLESPOON ALMOND FLOUR

1 LIGHT TABLESPOON SHREDDED COCONUT

1 teaspoon AGAVE

4 to 6 FRESH STRAWBERRIES, WASHED

In a small bowl, stir together the almond flour and coconut. Add the agave, then MIX AND MASH until it becomes a sticky paste. Bite the tip off a strawberry and use the rest to mop up some of the sweet mixture. REPEAT. REPEAT. REPEAT.

PLASTIC WRAPPERS AND PACKAGING CAN TAKE HUNDREDS OR THOUSANDS OF YEARS TO BREAK DOWN (AND THEY NEVER DISAPPEAR, BUT BREAK INTO SMALLER AND SMALLER PIECES THAT GET STUCK IN THE BELLIES OF BOTH LAND AND SEA ANIMALS). EAT FRESH, SHOP AT FARMERS' MARKETS, AND BUY WHAT YOU CAN FROM YOUR STORE'S BULK BINS TO CUT DOWN ON PLANET-POLLUTING TRASH AND CHEMICAL WASTE.

NOTE: You **MUST** have parchment or waxed paper and a very flat plate or piece of cardboard for this to work!

DISAPPEARING D*TS

MAKES ABOUT 20 DIME-SIZE DOTS

1 teaspoon COCONUT OIL, MELTED TO LIQUID

¼ TEASPOON aGAVE

¼ teaspoon Cacao POWDER

THEY MELT IN YOUR MOUTH!

Cover a small piece of sturdy cardboard or the flat part of a big plate with parchment or waxed paper. Tape down all sides so it doesn't curl up—you need a PERFECTLY flat surface! Then, in the teeniest bowl you can find, mix the ingredients together with a teaspoon (tip the bowl so the ingredients come together).

Using the TIP of the spoon (or a clean eyedropper if you have one), dab small dots (aim for the size of a dime, but smaller or bigger is okay, too) onto the parchment paper. Very slowly—and being careful not to tip it—put the cardboard or plate on a flat surface in the freezer for 5 minutes to harden the dots.

Enjoy them one by one as they disappear on your tongue, or drop them onto a scoop of vegan ice cream.

NO-BAKE CHOCOBALLS

MAKES ABOUT 10 ONE-INCH BALLS

¼ CUP ALMOND BUTTER

3 DATES (NO PITS!), CHOPPED
OR SNIPPED AS SMALL AS POSSIBLE

1½ TABLESPOONS CACAO POWDER

2 teaspoons AGAVE OR MAPLE SYRUP

OPTIONAL: ¼ teaspoon VANILLA EXTRACT,
a HANDFUL OF SHREDDED COCONUT for COATING

In a large sturdy bowl, mix and mash all ingredients using a wooden spoon. The longer you go, the smoother your "dough" will become, as you mash down the dates.

Once it's pretty smooth, pinch off small chunks, then roll and squish the dough into bite-size balls (wet your fingers with a bit of water if things get sticky). OPTIONAL: Place a handful of shredded coconut in a small bowl. Dip and roll some of the balls to coat the outsides.

Place them on a plate and chill in the freezer for 5 minutes before serving. Store extras in the fridge.

MOONDROPS
SESAME ALMOND COOKIES
MAKES 12 to 15 LiTTLE MARBLES

2-INCH-SQUARE PieCe of PLAiN NORi
1/2 CUP ALMOND FLOUR
1 TABLESPOON MAPLE SYRUP

2 teaSPOONS WATER
2 teaSPOONS RAW WHITE SESAME SEEDS

Preheat an oven to 300°F.

Fold and fold the nori into the smallest square you can. With clean scissors, snip tiny pieces off the corners, letting the shavings fall into a medium-size bowl.

Add all other ingredients and mix them into an even "dough" with a spoon. Pinch off small pieces of dough and form them into marble-size balls (wet your fingers in a little bowl of water if things get sticky—this REALLY helps form the dough). Place them on a cookie sheet lined with parchment paper and ADULT ALERT bake for 15 minutes or until they look toasty brown (keep your eyes on them near the end so they don't burn!).

Fresh out of the oven, Moondrops are lightly crisp on the outside, soft on the inside. Eat them warm, or let them cool, and they'll harden up a bit more.

YOU MIGHT HEAR THAT COW'S MILK IS GOOD FOR YOUR BONES, BUT THE COUNTRIES THAT DRINK THE MOST MILK HAVE THE MOST BONE DISEASE! TO GROW STRONG, YOUR BONES NEED CALCIUM AND MAGNESIUM. ALMONDS, SESAME SEEDS, AND SEAWEEDS ARE GOOD SOURCES OF BOTH (PLUS, CALCIUM FROM PLANTS IS EASIER FOR YOUR BODY TO SOAK UP).

DATES (pits removed) and/or FIGS

ALMONDS and/or CASHEWS
OR a NUT OF YOUR CHOICE

Push a nut into the center
of each fig or date, then
take the perfect bite!

SNUGGLE BUNNIES

WHEN YOU EAT SWEET FRUITS LIKE DATES AND FIGS, THE SUGAR THAT GOES INTO YOUR BODY COMES ALONG WITH VITAMINS AND MINERALS. BROWN AND WHITE SUGAR, ON THE OTHER HAND, ARE SEPARATED FROM THE PLANT'S NUTRIENTS, THEN WASHED, SPUN, DRIED, MIXED WITH CHEMICALS, AND OFTEN PASSED THROUGH ANIMAL BONE CHAR (BURNT BONES) TO REMOVE ANY COLOR (BROWN SUGAR IS JUST WHITE SUGAR MIXED WITH MOLASSES). EVERY BONE-CHAR FILTER USES ABOUT 7,800 COWS' BONES! WHICH SUGAR DO YOU THINK IS HEALTHIER FOR YOUR BODY, FOR ANIMALS, AND FOR THE EARTH?

Good things are worth waiting for. With just a jar, a few ingredients, and a little patience, you'll turn tough little chias into gooey, chewy gel bubbles with a pearly seed floating inside. This dessert recipe is also good for breakfast—just use less agave.

MUDPUDDLE

CHOCOLATE CHIA PUDDING
SERVES 1 or 2

> A MUDDY ANIMAL IS A WISE ANIMAL! WE USE MUD TO KEEP COOL AND PROTECT OUR SKIN FROM THE SUN.

1 CUP VEGAN MILK
(STORE-BOUGHT OR VERY NONDAIRY, PAGE 8)

¼ CUP CHIA SEEDS
(BE CAREFUL! DO NOT SPILL OR YOU'LL BE CLEANING UP FOR THE NEXT 10 YEARS!)

2 TABLESPOONS AGAVE

2 TEASPOONS CACAO POWDER

Put everything in a jar with a TIGHT cap, then SHAKE, SHAKE, SHAKE! SHAKE MORE! EVEN MORE! One more time! Let it sit in the fridge for at least 20 to 30 minutes (it'll get even more plump in a hour, even more over night!). Then stir really, really well, and if you'd like, add fruit, dried coconut, berries, or nuts on top. Chew, chew, chew those chias!

GREAT THINGS COME IN SMALL PACKAGES! PER GRAM, CHIA SEEDS CONTAIN ABOUT 5 TIMES MORE PROTEIN AND CALCIUM THAN MILK, ALMOST 3 TIMES MORE IRON THAN BEEF, 8 TIMES MORE OMEGA-3 THAN SALMON, PLUS ANTIOXIDANTS AND PHYTONUTRIENTS (SPECIAL NUTRIENTS FROM PLANTS).

Ancient Aztec people named chocolate a "FOOD FOR THE GODS." When you taste this little slice of heaven, you'll know why!

CHOCOLATE MOUSSE

MAKES ABOUT 1½ CUPS (SERVES 4 to 6)

2 AVOCADOS
(FRESHLY RIPE, <u>NOT</u> MUSHY!)

¼ CUP WATER <u>OR</u> VEGAN MILK
(STORE-BOUGHT OR VERY NONDAIRY, PAGE 8)

⅓ CUP CACAO POWDER

⅓ CUP AGAVE

OPTIONAL: A FEW DROPS of VANILLA EXTRACT

Scoop out the avo into a blender or food processor, add the liquid, and give it a quick whirl on low before adding the other ingredients. Blend everything together on low at first. If the machine gets stuck, stop to stir before blending again. Repeat until super smooth. Scoop it into a container with a lid and chill in the fridge before serving. Yummy with berries or sprinkled with shredded coconut, hemp seeds, or crushed nuts.

THE ANCIENT AZTEC PEOPLE OF MEXICO LOVED CHOCOLATE SO MUCH, THEY USED CACAO BEANS AS MONEY! THEIR GREAT EMPEROR MONTEZUMA KEPT **HEAPING MOUNTAINS** OF CACAO IN HIS TREASURE VAULTS.

NO-BAKE COCONUT
GRASS SHACKS

EACH RECIPE MAKES 6 to 8

CHOCOLATE:

½ CUP SHREDDED COCONUT

1½ TABLESPOONS COCONUT OIL
(MELTED to LIQUID)

2½ teaspoons AGAVE

2 teaspoons CACAO POWDER

A PINCH OF SALT

VANILLA:

½ CUP SHREDDED COCONUT

2 TABLESPOONS ALMOND FLOUR
(or ALMOND BUTTER, but the
shacks won't be as white)

1 TABLESPOON + 1 teaspoon COCONUT OIL
(MELTED to LIQUID)

2 teaspoons MAPLE SYRUP

¼ teaspoon VANILLA EXTRACT

2 DASHES of SALT

Pick a flavor, then mix and mash all ingredients REALLY WELL in a medium bowl. Cover a plate with parchment or waxed paper.

Have a little bowl of water nearby. Using a small spoon to scoop and your fingers to mold the shapes, form bite-size domes of your "dough" on the spoon. Dip your fingertips in the bowl of water in between each one so things don't get too sticky. (This REALLY helps the shacks take shape, too.) Very gently slide each dome off the spoon onto the plate. Put the plate in the freezer for 10 minutes to harden the shacks. Then gently twist the shacks loose—don't pull. Store leftovers in the fridge.

WHAT ELSE CAN WE DO?

- **DECORATE YOUR PLATE** Arrange the food in a pretty design or add a flower or a sprig of herbs.

- **MAKE HEALTHY EATING FUN!** Invite friends to help you cook and decorate the table with flowers, a houseplant, candles, ribbons, paper cutouts, or little animal figurines. You can even make your own placemats, menus, name cards, and seat assignments.

- **TAKE PICTURES** of the dishes you prepare! If you share them online, hashtag them #HelpYourselfCookbook.

- **BUY ORGANIC** as much as you can. Organic foods are grown without bug killers and weed killers, which pollute the Earth and make insects, animals, and people sick.

- **BRING YOUR OWN REUSABLE BAGS** whenever you go shopping.

• SHOP LOCAL Shopping for food and products grown or made nearby saves fuel, reduces plastic and packaging, benefits your neighborhood, local businesses, and farmers, and ensures that your food is as fresh as can be!

• KEEP A JAR OF COINS and add to it whenever you have loose change. At the end of the year, you can give the total to a good cause—human, animal, or Earth—and you will have helped someone who needed it.

• VISIT A PLANT NURSERY to learn how to grow a few pots of herbs so you always have them on hand for flavoring and tea.

• VISIT AN ANIMAL SANCTUARY OR RESCUE CENTER instead of the zoo. You'll learn about the real lives of animals—their joys and sorrows—and see that they have personalities, just like you.

• GET YOUR BARE FEET in the earth's soil as if you were a tree. You'll feel connected to the earth, breathe fresh air, and soak up the sun's energy.

• PLANT A TREE—even better, one that grows food. People who live in neighborhoods with trees feel safer, make friends with their neighbors, and feel more connected to the place they live. Nature is powerful!

SHOPPING LIST

PRODUCE SECTION (FRESH FOODS):

Apples
Artichokes
Asparagus
Avocados
Bananas
Basil, mint, and parsley (all fresh)
Beets
Blackberries, blueberries, strawberries
Broccoli
Carrots
Celery
Cucumbers
Garlic
Green onions
Kale
Lemons
Onions, red and yellow
Portobello mushrooms
Purple cabbage
Red bell peppers
Romaine or other lettuces or greens
Spinach
Tomatoes (small and big)
Yams
OPTIONAL: Cilantro, ginger, sprouts

DRY GOODS:

Almond flour
Cacao powder and nibs
Chia seeds
Coconut, dry (shredded and/or flakes)
Couscous
Dates
Dried fruit (apricots, figs, mango, pineapple)
Goji berries
Hemp seeds
Lentils (black, red)
Macadamia nuts
Oats, rolled
Popcorn kernels
Pumpkin seeds
Quinoa
Raisins (black, gold)
Raw almonds
Raw cashews
Raw sesame seeds ← store them in the refrigerator
Seaweed: Arame, hijiki, nori sheets and
    nori/laver pieces, roasted seaweed snacks
    (optional: kombu/kelp, palm, wakame)
Soba noodles
Walnuts
OPTIONAL: Pine nuts, pistachios

CANNED, JARRED, PREPARED:

Agave
Almond butter
Apple cider vinegar
Beans (black, garbanzo, pinto)
Chamomile tea bags
Hummus
Jam
Maple syrup
Mochi (try Grainaissance Original)
Mustard, Dijon
Sauerkraut
Stevia powder
Tahini
Tempeh (Lightlife Original or Three Grain)
Vegan cream cheese
Vegenaise ← *vegan mayo—in the refrigerated section of your grocery store*
OPTIONAL: Ketchup, olives

BREADS:

Sprouted grain tortillas (try Ezekiel 4:9)
Sprouted whole grain bread

BEVERAGES:

Coconut water
Vegan milk (almond, coconut, hemp, oat, rice, soy, etc.)

SEASONINGS:

Black pepper
Bragg Liquid Aminos (or shoyu)
Cinnamon
Cumin
Dried herb mix ← *Italian seasoning or herbes de Provence*
Nutritional yeast
Rapunzel's Vegetable Bouillon with Herbs and with Sea Salt
Sea salt
Turmeric
Vanilla extract

OILS:

Organic cold-pressed coconut oil
Organic cold-pressed olive oil

SUPPLEMENTS:

good for the immune system, brain, and overall health

Blue-green algae powder
Natren Mega Dophilus Non-Dairy Probiotics powder
Spirulina powder
OPTIONAL: Medicinal mushroom powder mix, vegan protein powder

RESOURCES

When you care about your health and about animals and the planet, it feels great to discover and support companies that are doing good work. With people and companies working together, we make the kind of world we WANT to live in. I like the food from the companies below, and I think you may, too.

NAVITAS NATURALS

This company cares about healthy food, habitats, the earth, and treating farmers fairly. It sells many of the superfoods we use in this book—cacao, goji berries, hemp seeds, coconut, cashews, and chia seeds—in organic versions grown without chemicals. They can be found in thousands of stores, including Whole Foods, health food stores, online, some Target stores, and even some Vons. www.navitasnaturals.com

FOLLOW YOUR HEART

This company is named after its owners' wish for the world. Not only do they make a super tasty vegan mayonnaise called Vegenaise (it's so good you'll want to eat it by itself—try dipping veggies in it!), as well as lots of other vegan cheeses and products, they use the power of the sun to do it! From their use of solar energy to their special factory full of recycled materials, they try to do business in environmentally friendly ways. Good name for a good company, right? You can find their mayonnaise in the refrigerated section of most health food stores. www.followyourheart.com

NUTREX HAWAII

This company grows its spirulina in areas protected from chemical pollution. You can find its Pure Hawaiian Spirulina Pacifica at Whole Foods, most health food stores, or online. www.nutrex-hawaii.com/hawaiian-spirulina-pacifica

IF YOUR LOCAL GROCERY STORE DOESN'T CARRY THESE ITEMS YET, SIMPLY ASK THEM TO! STORES WANT TO SELL WHAT THEIR CUSTOMERS WANT TO BUY!

HEALTHFORCE NUTRITIONALS

One of my most favorite companies in the world for nutritious powders! It is owned by the super-energetic vegan Dr. Jameth Sheridan, who loves helping people get the healthiest, most powerful, and most pure ingredients there are. (He calls them "TruGanic," even PURER than organic, and puts them in recyclable glass bottles, too!) I love HealthForce's Spirulina Azteca powder, Truly Natural Vitamin C powder, Elixir of the Lake blue-green algae, Green Protein Alchemy Mint Magic Mint green powder, and vegan protein powders, too.
www.healthforce.com

NATREN PROBIOTICS

Probiotics are the teeny tiny nutrients in fermented (aged) foods that travel through your belly and digestive system to keep your whole body healthy and balanced. A half teaspoon of a probiotic powder can contain two billion nutrients—whoa! Many probiotics are made from animal dairy products, but Natren makes an all-vegan powder that has no taste at all—great for mixing into smoothies. You can buy its Megadophilus or Healthy Trinity dairy-free powders loose or in capsules (you can pull the capsules apart and pour the contents into your recipes). NOTE: Good probiotics are very delicate and must be kept cold, so look for them in the refrigerated section of your health food store.
www.natren.com

RAPUNZEL

Rapunzel is a company that works very hard to protect the land, habitats, and farmers who grow its ingredients. I really love its bouillon cubes with sea salt or herbs because they help make soups super flavorful in just minutes. Read about Rapunzel's planet-saving practices here: www.rapunzel.de/uk

THE END

(OR JUST THE BEGINNING)

THANK YOU!

JUSTIN AND AKIRA BUA for inspiring and supporting everything I do; LYNN AND ANDY ROTH for unwavering encouragement; MARILYN ALLEN for never giving up; my awesome editor, GRACE SUH, for pushing this project and for so much freedom and fun; my food stylist, ALICIA BUSZCZAK, and my photographer, JENNIFER CHONG, for being the best, most patient team ever; JULIE MORRIS, MARK LEITNER AND THE NAVITAS NATURALS TEAM for the incredible support; my sister CHLOE ROTH for her assistance (and comedy relief) during our photo shoot; ELE KEATS, ANNE SAGE, REBECCA BUENIK, DARIN CHAVEZ, the Hollywood Farmer's Market, JACOB RUSHING for my author photo, my supportive readers, and all those whose efforts and LOVE are changing the world.

INDEX

123

RUBY ROTH

is an artist, designer, activist, and the world's leading author and illustrator of vegan and vegetarian books for children. She has been featured on many major media outlets, including the TODAY show, CNN, ABC, FOX, WIRED, REDBOOK, and GLAMOUR.

A former elementary school art teacher, Ruby was inspired by her students to write children's picture books on veganism, which have since been translated into multiple languages. Roth lives in Los Angeles with her artist beau and 11-year-old stepdaughter, who loves to cook. They are all healthy, happy vegans.

SHOP, BLOG, AND
NEWSLETTER—COME VISIT!

WWW.WEDONTEATANIMALS.COM

WWW.FACEBOOK.COM/WEDONTEATANIMALS

@RUBY_ROTH
@WEDONTEATANIMALS

@RUBY_ROTH

OTHER BOOKS BY
RUBY ROTH

V Is for Vegan
The ABCs of Being Kind

Written and Illustrated by Ruby Roth
author of That's Why We Don't Eat Animals and Vegan Is Love

That's Why We
Don't Eat Animals
A Book About Vegans, Vegetarians,
and All Living Things

Written and Illustrated
by Ruby Roth

Vegan Is Love
Having Heart and Taking Action

Written & Illustrated by
Ruby Roth

Andrews McMeel Publishing
a division of Andrews McMeel Universal
1130 Walnut Street, Kansas City, Missouri 64106

www.andrewsmcmeel.com

16 17 18 19 20 TEN 10 9 8 7 6 5 4 3 2

ISBN: 978-1-4494-7187-3

Library of Congress Control Number: 2015950111

Editor: Grace Suh
Designer: Ruby Roth
Photographer: Jennifer Chong
Photo Stylist: Alicia Buszczak
Art Director: Julie Barnes
Copy Chief: Maureen Sullivan
Production Manager: Carol Coe
Demand Planner: Sue Eikos

Photography on pages 126-127 by Jacob Rushing.

ATTENTION: SCHOOLS AND BUSINESSES
Andrews McMeel books are available at quantity discounts with bulk purchase for educational, business, or sales promotional use. For information, please e-mail the Andrews McMeel Publishing Special Sales Department: specialsales@amuniversal.com.